LUDWIG von MISES ON MONEY AND INFLATION

A Synthesis of Several Lectures

LUDWIG von MISES
ON
MONEY AND INFLATION

A Synthesis of Several Lectures

By Ludwig von Mises
Compiled by Bettina Bien Greaves

Ludwig von Mises Institute
AUBURN, ALABAMA

10 9 8 7 6 5 4 3 2 1

Ludwig von Mises Institute
518 West Magnolia Avenue
Auburn, Alabama 36832

mises.org

ISBN: 978-1-933550-75-6

CONTENTS

Introduction

Upon the establishment of the Foundation for Economic Education (FEE) in 1946, Ludwig von Mises became a part-time adviser, and he served in that capacity until his death in 1973. Whenever FEE held a seminar in Irvington, if he was in town he would drive out from New York City, where he lived with his wife, Margit, to speak to the participants. His topic was quite often inflation. I attended all those lectures, took them down in shorthand and later transcribed them. The thought occurred to me that eight to ten of his lectures on inflation, delivered in the 1960s, might be integrated, with the duplications deleted, and turned into a single piece. Hence this paper.

Mises did not like to have his oral remarks quoted or published because, obviously, they did not represent the care and precision he devoted to his writings. However, it does not seem to me that these lectures, as I have edited them, misrepresent his ideas in any way. Moreover, they reveal his unpretentious manner and the informal simple style he used when talking to students. He often rephrased an idea in several different ways, repeating it for emphasis. He was frequently accused of being "simplistic," of making economic subjects appear too clear and simple, but it was this very approach that made it possible for persons, even those without any background in economics, to understand and appreciate what he was saying.

Bettina Bien Greaves

CHAPTER

ONE

Human Cooperation

Human cooperation is different from the activities that took place under prehuman conditions in the animal kingdom and among isolated persons or groups during the primitive ages. The specific human faculty that distinguishes man from animal is cooperation. Men cooperate. That means that, in their activities, they anticipate that activities on the part of other people will accomplish certain things in order to bring about the results they are aiming at with their own work. The market is that state of affairs under which I am giving something *to* you in order to receive something *from* you. I don't know how many of you have some inkling, or idea, of the Latin language, but in a Latin pronouncement 2,000 years ago already, there was the best description of the market—*do ut des*—I give in order that you should give. I contribute something in order that you should contribute something else. Out of this there developed human society, the market, peaceful cooperation of individuals. Social cooperation means the division of labor.

The various members, the various individuals, in a society do not live their own lives without any reference or connection with other individuals. Thanks to the division of labor, we are connected with others by working for them and by receiving and consuming what others have produced for us. As a result, we have an exchange economy which consists in the cooperation of many individuals. Everybody produces, not only for himself alone, but for other people in the expectation that these other people will produce for him. This system requires acts of exchange.

The peaceful cooperation, the peaceful achievements of men are effected on the market. Cooperation necessarily means that people are exchanging services and goods, the products of services. These exchanges bring about the market. The market is precisely the freedom of people to produce, to consume, to determine what has to be produced, in whatever quantity, in whatever quality, and to whomever these products are to go. Such a free system without a market is impossible; such a free system *is* the market.

We have the idea that the institutions of men are either (1) the market, exchange between individuals, or (2) the government, an institution which, in the minds of the many people, is something superior to the market and could exist in the absence of the market. The truth is that the government—that is the recourse to violence, necessarily the recourse to violence—cannot produce anything. Everything that is produced is produced by the activities of individuals and is used on the market in order to receive something in exchange for it.

It is important to remember that everything that is done, everything that man has done, everything that society does, is the result of such voluntary cooperation and agreements. Social cooperation among men—and this means the market—is what brings about civilization and it is what has brought about all the improvements in human conditions we are enjoying today.

CHAPTER
TWO

The Medium of Exchange—Money

The definition of money is very simple. Money is the general medium of exchange used on the market. Money, the medium of exchange, is something that individuals choose in order to facilitate the exchange of commodities. Money is a market phenomenon. What does that mean? It means that money developed on the market, and that its development and its functioning have nothing to do with the government, the state, or with the violence exercised by governments.

The market developed what is called indirect exchange. The man who couldn't get what he wanted on the market through direct exchange, through barter, took something else, something that was considered more easily negotiable, something which he expected to trade later for what he really wanted. The market, the people on the market, the people in organizing the division of labor and bringing about the system in which one man produces shoes and another produces coats, brought about the system in which coats can be exchanged against shoes, but only practically on account of the difference of the importance and the value, by the intermediary of money. Thus the market system made it possible for people who could not get today what they needed, what they wanted to buy on the market, to take, in return for what they brought to trade, a medium of exchange—that means something that was more easily used on the market than what they brought to the market to exchange. With a medium of exchange, the originators of the exchange can attain satisfaction finally by acquiring those things which they themselves want to consume.

Money is a medium of exchange because people use it as such. People don't eat the money; they ask for the money because they want to use it to give it away in a new contract. And this barter or trade is technically possible only if there is a medium of exchange, a money, against which he can exchange what he has for the things he wants and needs. All the mutual givings and receivings that take place on the market, all these mutual exchanges that lead to the development of money, are the voluntary achievements of individual people.

Through a long evolution, governments, or certain groups of governments, have promoted the idea that money is not simply a market phenomenon, but that it is whatever the government calls money. But money is not what the government says. The idea of money is that it is a medium of exchange; somebody who sells something and is not in a position to exchange again immediately for the thing he wants to consume gets something else which he can exchange for this at a later date. This "something else" is a medium of exchange, because the man who sells, let us say, chickens or eggs, does not, or cannot get directly what he wants himself to consume, but must take something else which he uses at a later date in order to get what he needs.

If people say that money is not the most important thing in the world, they may be perfectly right from the point of view of the ideas that are responsible for the conduct of human affairs. But if they say that money is not important, they do not understand what money does. Money, the medium of exchange, makes it possible for everybody to attain what he wants by exchanging again and again. He may not acquire directly the things he wants to consume. But money makes it easier for the individual to satisfy his needs through other exchanges. In other words, people first exchange what they have produced, for a medium of exchange, something which is more easily exchangeable than what they have produced; then through later exchanges, they are able to acquire the things they want to consume. And this is the service which money renders to the economic system; it makes it easier for people to acquire the things they want and need.

CHAPTER
THREE

The Role of the Courts and Judges

Government interference with the market and with money occurs only in cases in which individuals are not prepared to do what they voluntarily promised to do. Having chosen for himself the field in which he wants to work, he must barter or trade what he himself has produced in order to survive, in order to obtain the things he needs to live. If the acts of exchange are such that not everybody gives and receives the goods and services contracted for at the same time, difficulties can arise. The value and the meaning of the things which are given away and those which are received are never equal or identical, not only in size and quality but also, what is still more important, as to the time period over which an exchange is to be carried out.

If people enter into a contract, if both parties decide that something must be done immediately, there is as a rule no reason for any disagreement between the parties. Both parties to the exchange receive immediately the thing they want to acquire for what they give away. The whole act of exchange is then finished; there are no further consequences. But most exchanges are not of this kind. In reality there are many exchanges wherein both parties do not have to deliver immediately what they are obligated to deliver. If the parties to a contract, to an exchange, want to postpone the settlement, the execution, of their contract, differences of opinion can arise, some very serious differences of opinion, concerning the correctness of one or the other party's contribution. Translated from the more abstract language used by lawyers and economists, that means that if one man has entered into a contract with another man wherein he has promised to do something at a later date, the question may arise when that time comes whether this promise was really executed correctly according to the tenets of the contract.

Money is a medium of exchange, a phenomenon that developed out of the market. Money is the result of an historical evolution that, in the course of many hundreds and thousands of years brought about the use of exchange through the intermediary of a medium of exchange. Money is the generally accepted and generally used medium of exchange; it is not something created by the government; it is something created by the people buying and selling on the market. But if people don't comply with their voluntarily accepted agreements, then the government has to interfere. And in any interference of the government, the government has to find out before it interferes whether there really was a violation of voluntarily entered contracts. Such contracts are the results of agreements, and if the people do not comply with what they have promised then it is the state that has to interfere in order to prevent individuals from resorting to violence. The government is called on to protect the market against people who don't want to comply with the obligations which they have to fulfill under the market, and among these obligations is the obligation of making payments in definite sums of money. If somebody wants to appeal for government interference against other people because these other people failed to comply with what they had accepted voluntarily as an agreement, then it is the duty of the government, of the courts, of the judges, to determine what money is and what it is not. Now what governments did, what governments had done for thousands of years, we could say, is to misuse the position this gives them in order to declare as money what is *not* money, or what has a lower purchasing power per individual piece.

The market, the real social institution, the fundamental social institution, has one terrific weakness. The weakness is not in the institution of the market but in the human beings who are operating on the market. There are people who do not want to comply with the fundamental principle of the market—voluntary agreement and action according to voluntary agreement. There are people who resort to violence. And there are people who do not comply with the obligations which they have voluntarily accepted in agreement with other people. The market, the fundamental human social institution cannot exist if there is not an institution that protects it against those people who either resort to violence or who are not prepared to comply with the obligations which they have voluntarily accepted. This institution is the state, the police power of the state, the power to resort to violence in order to prevent other people, ordinary men, from resorting to violence.

Now, violence is a bad thing. The fact that violence is necessary, that it is indispensable in some situations, such as in settling disputes concerning contracts, does not make the institution imposing the violence, the government, a good institution. Nevertheless, the idea prevails, more or less throughout the whole world that, on the one hand, government, the institution that resorts to violence, is a great and a good thing, and that, on the other hand, the market, the system of voluntary social cooperation, though perhaps necessary—although most people don't even realize this—is certainly not something which must be considered good.

Now everything that human action has achieved is the outcome of the voluntary cooperation of men. What the government does, or what the government ought to do, is to protect these activities from people who do not comply with the rules that are necessary for the preservation of human society and all that it produces. As a matter of fact, the government's main function, or let us say even its *only* function, is to preserve the system of voluntary action or cooperation among people by preventing people from resorting to violence. What the government has to do with respect to this medium of exchange is only to prevent people from refusing to comply with the commitments they have made. This is *not* a function of building something; it is a function of protecting those who are building.

Among the things refractory individuals sometimes do is to fail to fulfill their obligations under market agreements. To say it very simply, an individual made an agreement, and yet this individual does not comply with his obligations under that agreement. Then it is necessary to resort to government action. What can you do if the other party to an agreement says, "Yes, I know. I received something from you under an agreement by which I was bound to give you something in exchange. But I shan't give it to you. I am a bad man. What can you do about it? You must just grin and bear it." Or it is possible that the person who has to deliver at a later time says, "I'm sorry but I cannot, or I will not, deliver." This makes the whole market system of exchanges, the whole system based upon the voluntary actions of individuals, break down.

If a man has offered in a contract to deliver potatoes in three months, for instance, the question may come up when he delivers whether what he gives the buyer really is potatoes in the meaning of the contract. The party who was bound to deliver potatoes may have delivered something that the second party does not consider potatoes. Then the second party says, "When we made an agreement concerning potatoes we had something else in mind. We had something in mind that had certain qualities which these potatoes don't have." Then it is the duty of the government, of the judge whom the government appoints for this purpose, to find out whether or not these questionable potatoes are really what was understood by the contracting parties to be "potatoes." They must not be spoiled; they must be of a certain character; they must be potatoes according to commercial usage; and so on. They may be potatoes from the point of view of a professor of botany but not potatoes from the point of view of the businessman. This is something which trade usage determines everywhere. The judge cannot be familiar with everything that is going on in the world and, therefore, he very often needs the advice of an expert. The expert must say whether or not the potatoes in question should really be considered the kind of potatoes meant in the agreement. And then it is the business of the judge to consider the expert's advice and to determine whether what has been delivered really is potatoes or whether they are something else.

Agreements concerning products such as potatoes—or anything else for that matter, wheat, for instance—which are made regularly on the market through the intermediary of a medium of exchange, popularly called "money," can be violated, as we have seen, on the commodity side. But they can also be violated on the side of the money. That means that a conflict, a difference of opinion, may arise between the two parties to a contract concerning the money which has to be paid to comply with the contract. And then the government, the judges, must determine whether what is offered under the name of money in this case is really what the people had in mind when they made the contract. Government was not directly involved in the development of money; the task of the government in this connection is simply to see that people *fulfill* the terms of their contracts with respect to the money. Just as the judge can say what is, or what is not, meant in the contract by the term "potatoes" or "wheat," so under special conditions, to preserve peaceful conditions in the country, the judge must determine what was meant when the parties to a contract mentioned "money." What did the people use as a medium of exchange? What did they have in mind in their contract when they said, "I will pay you certain units of 'money' when you do what you have promised." Whether these units are called dollars, or thalers, or marks, or pounds doesn't matter; the government has only to find out what the meaning of the contract was.

This is what government has to decide. The government does not have the power to call something "money" which the parties didn't have in mind as money when concluding their contract any more than it has the power to call non-potatoes "potatoes," or to call a piece of iron, let us say, "copper." It is *not* that the government says what money is originally; it is just that it must say what is meant by "money" in the case of the contract that is in conflict. I have to say all these things in order to point out something people do not seem to know today, namely that money is *not* created by government. People today don't know this because the étatist, statist, ideas about the market and about money have destroyed knowledge of how money is created.

It is only in dealing with the problem of whether or not the money obligations in contracts have been filled that the government or, let us say, the judge, has anything to say about money. It is only in this way that the government comes into touch, originally into touch, with money—just as it comes into touch with everything else, that is with potatoes, wheat, apples, motor cars, and so on. Therefore, it is not true that money is something derived from the government, that the government is sovereign with regard to money, and that it can say what money is. It is not true that the government's relationship to money is different from what it is to other things. Money is a product of market agreements just as is everything else that enters into exchange agreements.

If a judge were to say that whatever the government calls a horse is whatever the government calls a horse, and that the government has the right to call a chicken a horse, everybody would consider him either corrupt or insane. Yet in the course of a very long evolution, the government has converted the situation that the government must settle disputes concerning the meaning of "money" as referred to in contracts, into another situation. Over centuries many governments and many theories of law have brought about the doctrine that money, one side of most exchange agreements, is whatever the government calls money. The governments are pretending to have the right to do what this doctrine tells them, that is to declare anything, even a piece of paper, "money." And this is the root of the monetary problem.

This makes it possible to do anything with money, to falsify it, or to debase it, in any way you want so long as you have the government, its judges and its executioners on your side. And therefore a system developed which is very well known to everybody. The government presumes that it is the government's right, duty and privilege to declare what money is and to manufacture this money. This system brings about a situation in which it is possible for the government to do anything it wants, anything that can be done with money. And this creates a situation in which the government uses its power to print and to coin money for such purposes as increasing the means, the purchasing power, with which it appears on the market.

CHAPTER
FOUR

Gold as Money

Now, we must realize that historically people everywhere used at the beginning a definite type of commodity as a medium of exchange. Sometimes you find mentioned in books what kinds of goods and commodities were used in different countries at different ages as a general medium of exchange, as money. People once chose various kinds of commodities as media of exchange, as intermediaries between sellers and buyers. These commodities which they chose were commodities which were available in limited quantities only. If something is available in sufficient quantity to meet all possible kinds of demand, or can be increased in quantity in such a way as to meet all possible kinds of demand, then it doesn't have any value in exchange. *Only something that is available in a limited quantity can have exchange value, can be considered as valuable by people.*

Over centuries traders eliminated everything else from among the various articles and commodities used as media of exchange until only the precious metals—gold and silver—remained. All other commodities were eliminated as media of exchange. When I say that the other things were eliminated from being used as money, what I mean is that people in making agreements eliminated them; people in making agreements rejected other things as media of exchange and turned to using only gold and silver; they specified gold and silver in the contracts they made when trading with other parties. Thus we must realize that the evolution to gold and silver money was brought about by private persons. Then silver also disappeared as a medium of exchange in the last centuries and the fact remained that the commodity gold was used as the medium of exchange. The function of the government consisted of producing small pieces of this medium of exchange, the weight and content of which was determined by the government offices and acknowledged by the laws and by the courts. I cannot enter into the whole history of money. But what resulted was the gold standard. The system of the gold standard, the gold exchange standard, is practically the only monetary system in the world. This was not done by governments; it was done through the market; it was done by parties exchanging on the market.

In the history of money, which is identical with the history of government attempts to destroy money, we must distinguish two great periods. And these two periods are not separated from one another by some monetary fact or by some specific monetary problem—they are separated from one another by the great invention made in the 15th century by a man named Gutenberg. If the governments need more money—and they always need more money because they don't earn it—the simplest way for them to increase the quantity of money since Gutenberg is just to print it.

Just as the government says "dollar"—but let us not use the term of a country with money which still functions today—let us say "ducats." You have agreed upon a definite quantity of ducats. And then, because the government doesn't want to restrict its expenditures, it declares: "What I have printed in my printing office, in my government printing office and called a Ducat is also a Ducat, the same thing as a gold Ducat." These things started when there were private banks to which the government gave privileges. At the time you made this agreement a Ducat meant a definite quantity of gold. But the government now says it is something else. When the government does this, the situation is similar to what it would be if you agreed to deliver a horse to another party but instead of a horse you delivered a chicken, saying, "This is all right … I say that this chicken means a horse." It is such a system that destroys the markets, you know.

I want to say something about the reason why the gold standard was adopted in the first place and also why today it is considered as the only really sound system of money. It is because gold alone makes the determination of the purchasing power of the monetary unit independent of the changes in ideas of governments and political parties. Gold has one advantage. It cannot be printed. It cannot be increased *ad libitum* [at pleasure]. If you think that you, or an institution with which you are connected doesn't have enough gold money, you cannot do anything about it that would increase the quantity of gold money in a very simple and cheap way. The reason why there is the gold standard, why the gold standard was accepted, is that an increase in the quantity of gold costs money. Gold is restricted; it is limited by nature; the production of an additional quantity of gold is not cheaper than the acquisition of such a quantity by exchanges on the market. That means that the metal gold was used as a medium of exchange.

Governments and writers for governments make fun of the fact that the world, the nations of the world, consider gold as money. They say a lot of things against the gold standard. But what they say is not what matters. What matters is that, without any interference on the part of a central authority, without any government action, individuals chose gold as "money" through the process of trading on the market. People make jokes about the uselessness of gold. It is just a silly yellow metal. We can't eat it, they say. It is only good for dentists and for unimportant things like jewelry. There are people who say, "Why gold? Why use precisely this yellow metal as money? Leave the gold to the dentists. Don't use it for monetary purposes." Now I do not have the right to talk about the dentists; I use the dentists only as an illustration. Whether *they* want the gold is another question. Lord Keynes called the gold standard a "barbarous relic." Many books say that the government had to step in because the gold standard failed. But the gold standard didn't fail! The government abolished the gold standard by making it illegal to hold gold. But still today, all international trade is calculated in gold. Critics have no valid arguments against the gold standard because the gold standard works while the paper standard of the government does not work, not even in a way which the government itself considers satisfactory.

The advantage of this gold money system, as of every system of non-governmental money, is that an increase in the quantity of money does not depend on decisions of the government. The advantage of the gold standard is that the quantity of gold available is independent of the actions, the wishes, the projects and, I would say, of the "crimes," of the various governments. Gold may not be an ideal money, certainly not; there are no ideals in the world of reality. But we can use gold as a medium of exchange because the quantity of gold is by and large limited and the production of additional quantities requires expenditures that do not influence the purchasing power of the already existing gold to a greater extent than such changes are occurring daily again and again in everything. We can therefore live, we can therefore exist, with the system of gold money. With gold money, there is no danger that a great revolution in prices will be brought about. The advantage of the gold standard is not that gold is yellow and shiny and heavy, but on account of the fact that the production of gold, like the production of everything else, depends on actors who cannot be manipulated by the government in the way in which the government can manipulate the production of government paper money. When the government prints a piece of paper, it doesn't cost more to print "100" than it does to print "10" or "1" on this same piece of paper. And the market situation, the situation for all human exchanges, the whole economic system is undermined, destroyed, by the governments when they consider it advisable to increase the quantity of money by increasing the quantity of government money.

The monetary crisis, the monetary problem which faces the world today is due to the fact that the governments think they are free to do anything they want with regard to money, you know. Not only do individuals sometimes fail to fulfill promises they have made, but governments do the same. They have already used practically all possible methods of trying to evade the necessity of paying what they have promised. And this is the problem which we have now.

Legal tender legislation made it impossible for anybody to refuse to accept the paper money. Gold clauses were written into some contracts by some people in the attempt to protect them against the legal tender laws which would force them to accept paper. To give an example, there is a country in Europe, a very nice country with a great history, considered even today as one of the most civilized countries of the world. I don't want to give the name of the nation, but let us call it Utopia.[1] This country issued a loan, a public loan. On every page of this loan there was inscribed: "This government promises to pay 20 pieces of Utopian gold money, that is a definite quantity of gold coins in the coinage of this nation, that amount in gold, or an equivalent quantity in American dollars redeemable in gold according to the McKinley standard." The man who bought this obligation, this letter of indebtedness, would have said: "I am really protected against all accidents. It has happened in the past that a country did not pay the same weight of gold which it had promised to pay. But now I have the promise not only of being paid in gold, but I also have the power to choose. I can ask them to pay me in the Utopian national currency, or the equivalent in American dollars, which are redeemable in gold." Then in 1933 the United States changed the "price" of gold, as you

[1] Speaking on another occasion (April 30, 1953 at his NYU seminar), Mises was not so discreet; there he identified the country whose bonds he was discussing as Sweden. —BBG

know; it reduced the ratio of gold to the U.S. dollar. In 1935 the U.S. Supreme Court ruled[2] that, as the bondholders had received payment in legal tender notes, they could not show damage and would not be paid in gold. This country of Utopia said, "We also accept this new 'price.' We will pay you, the bondholder, only the lower quantity of gold according to the new American law, a law which didn't exist at the time we sold you this obligation when we bound ourselves to pay to you." That means the right of governments concerning money is considered as something quite special today, something which is not subject to the general conditions and practices of the market economy. This precisely is the reason for the monetary problem which we now have.

All this was possible only on account of the fact that government is the institution that determines what the agreements between the citizens mean, what the content of these agreements are. Government has the power to force people who, according to their government's declaration, do not comply with their agreement to pay the sums required. And as the government assumes, necessarily, that the courts should have the power to declare whether or not the parties have complied with an agreement concluded between them, so do the governments presume that they alone have the power to declare what money is and what money is not. Just as the courts have to determine if there is a conflict between the parties to an agreement as to whether a certain thing referred to in a contract is wool, for instance, or is not wool, so do the governments presume to say whether a certain thing is money or is not money of a certain definite quantity. And in this way, again and again, governments have destroyed the markets of the world. And in destroying the markets they have gone so far as to destroy completely the system of money, making it necessary to develop a new monetary system.

What we have to realize is this: Every kind of human arrangement is connected in some way or other with money payments. And, therefore if you destroy the monetary system of a country or of the whole world, you are destroying much more than simply one aspect. When you destroy the monetary system, you are destroying in some regards the basis of all interhuman relations. If one talks of money, one talks about a field in which governments were doing the very worst thing which could be done, destroying the market, destroying human cooperation, destroying

[2] The majority of the Court found on February 18, 1935 in the Gold Clause cases that the plaintiffs had not been harmed by the abrogation of the gold clause because they did not show that in relation to buying power they had sustained any loss whatsoever. —**BBG**

all peaceful relations between men.

The fact is that with the gold standard it is possible to have a monetary standard that cannot be destroyed by the governments. There is no reason to give to the governments greater influence over monetary problems. While it is really absolutely correct to say that it is just an accident that it is precisely gold and not something else that serves this monetary purpose, the fact is that with the gold standard it is impossible for governments to destroy the monetary system. On the other hand, *there is nothing easier for governments to do than to destroy a system of money which is based upon too much confidence in the government.*

CHAPTER
FIVE

Gold Inflation

The gold standard is due to an accident, a geological accident, I would say, that there is only a limited quantity available. Because its quantity is limited, it has value on the market so that we can deal with it as money. The main thing with regard to money is the question, how to restrict, how not to increase, its quantity.

You know gold too can increase in quantity even if you have the gold standard. In the last 200 years it happened again and again that the increase, that the discovery of new fields in which gold, additional quantities of gold, could be produced, brought about a slight drop in the purchasing power of every gold unit as against the purchasing power of the gold unit which would have remained in the absence of this new discovery. This same tendency toward higher prices was then brought about not only by an increase in the quantity of paper money but also by an increase in the quantity of precious metals. For instance, in the years 1848 to 1849, there was discovered gold in California and Australia. For a definite period a new quantity of gold, above the regular yearly increase in the production of gold, was flowing into the market. Lots of people went to these gold fields, tried to mine gold, and when they did find gold they spent it. The result, therefore, was that these gold miners took away from the markets more produced goods than they had taken before.

If, for instance, a poor man, who had not formerly consumed very much, went to California or Australia, and had some success in gold mining, he was then able to buy things with his gold and to live in a very comfortable manner. Within a very short time, within a few months or years, there developed towns in California, places where the gold miners lived very agreeable lives. The gold miners received in exchange for the gold real things. Where only a short time before there had been nothing but forests and swamps, there were cities, houses, furniture and imported bottles of champagne. And where did all these things come from? From the rest of the world. And what did the rest of the world, the producers and suppliers of the goods and services get in exchange for the things the gold miners bought? Higher prices! They received gold, of course, but they had to pay more for the things they wanted to buy. The effect of these great gold discoveries was that the purchasing power of each individual piece of gold was now lower than it would have been in the absence of the gold discoveries. You can, if you want, call it "inflation;" it brought about effects similar to those of a paper money inflation.

That is, in the middle of the 19th century the new gold discoveries brought about what people considered at that time as a price revolution, or something like that. But the production of additional money, gold money, was limited; it was almost without any quantitative influence upon the great markets of the whole world. When the only real money which was used was gold money or bills which were redeemable, convertible into gold, bills giving you the right to get a quantity of money, then as the quantity of gold was increasing, there was a drop in its purchasing power. And adjustments were taking place which were necessary in order to bring this in order. But this drop in purchasing power was limited because the additional quantities of gold were very soon integrated into the whole monetary system and there were no farther extraordinary increases in the quantity of money. Now these gold discoveries are exceptional cases and we do not have to deal with them.

People may make jokes about the gold standard, suggesting that one should leave the gold to the dentists, that gold is absolutely unnecessary for money, and that besides it is a waste of money and work to use as money something that has to be produced at such a high cost as gold. But the gold standard has one quality, one virtue; it is that gold cannot be printed, and that gold cannot be produced in a cheaper way by any governmental committee, institution, office, international office, or so on. This is the *only* justification for the gold standard. One has tried again and again to find some method to substitute these qualities of gold in some other way. But all these methods have failed, and will ever fail precisely as long as the governments are committed to the idea that it is all right for a government that has not collected enough money to pay its expenses by taxing its citizens, or from borrowing on the market, that it is all right for such a government to increase the quantity of money simply by printing it.

Now there is a doctrine that says there is not enough gold. The reason why these critics of gold are against the gold standard is due to their belief that the quantity of money must be increased. Now the quantity of money adjusts itself necessarily through prices to the demands of the public. Yet, there are authors, professors, textbook writers, who tell us there is not enough money and they suggest a paper currency and regular yearly increases in the quantity of money. They don't know what they are talking about. Some of these textbook authors give another figure in every new edition of their textbooks by which they want to increase the quantity of money. In one edition they say 5%, in the next edition they say 8%, and so on. If a professor says that we should have a paper currency and that every year the government should add 8%, or 10%, or 5% additional new money, he does not give us a full description of what has to be done. This is perhaps an interesting fact to help us realize, let us say, the mentality of these authors, but it is not the problem which we have to deal with. The question is *how* the government should bring this money into circulation, to whom should it be given. What we have to realize is that the increase in the quantity of money cannot be neutral with regard to the conditions of the various individuals.

It is, of course, rather puzzling that one has no other method of organizing the system of exchanges than by the use of a definite metal, a yellow metal, gold. One may ask the question: "What would have happened if there hadn't been any gold?" Or one may ask the question: "What will happen one day," nobody can say anything today about it, "if people discover a method to produce gold at such a cheap price that gold will no longer be useful for the monetary purpose?" To this question, I answer: "Ask me again when this is the case." Perhaps—I don't know, nobody knows—perhaps one day people will discover a method of producing gold out of nothing, or, let us say, out of non-gold. Perhaps gold will become as plentiful as air, and free to everyone. If everyone could have as much gold as he wanted, it would have no value on the market. No one would then be willing to take such a value-less commodity in trade for other goods or services and it would not then become a "medium of exchange." If you have sleepless nights and have nothing else to think about, you could think about what will happen, you know, if one day gold could be produced in such a cheap way as, let us say, paper can be produced today. It *could* happen! But nobody thinks it will happen. It probably will not happen. But if it does happen then people will have to deal with the new problem.

And perhaps they will solve it; perhaps they will not solve it; we don't know that today. But it is useless today to speculate what will happen, if this should happen. And as we don't know anything about what the conditions will be at that time, we can say, "Let us wait. Let us wait to see whether really one day gold will be so abundant that it can no longer serve monetary purposes." All right. If this should happen, the people living then—at that time—would have a problem to solve. But today we have another problem. Our problem is to keep the quantity of money from being increased and its purchasing power from being decreased through inflation.

CHAPTER
SIX

Inflation

The first rule, or the only rule which we have to teach to everybody in explaining the problems of money is that an increase in the quantity of money brings about for the group, for the people, for the society, for the king, for the emperor who does it, a temporary improvement of the situation. But if so, why do it today only and not repeat it tomorrow? This is the only question. And this is the problem of inflation.

The problem is not to increase the quantity of money. The problem is to increase the quantity of those things which can be bought with money. And if you are increasing the quantity of money, and you are not increasing the quantity of things which can be bought with money, you are only increasing the prices which are paid for them. And in time, if the increase in money continues, the whole system becomes a system without any meaning and really without any possible method of dealing with it.

Unfortunately we are living in a period in which many governments say, if we don't have enough money for something and if we don't want to tax people because the people don't want to pay taxes for this purpose, then let us add a little bit, a little bit of paper money, not very much, just a little bit, you know. I would like to attack the problem from another point of view and say: "There is nothing in the world *less* fit to serve as money than paper, printed paper." Nothing is cheaper. And practically what we have to say is that the governments are destroying the whole economic system of the market economy by destroying the monetary system. One could compare this printing of paper money, and people have, with what has happened in the field of the use of various drugs. Just as when you start to use certain drugs you don't know when to stop nor how to stop, it is the same with the printing of paper money, the governments don't know when nor how to stop.

Prices are going up because there is an additional quantity of money, asking, searching for a not-increased quantity of commodities. And the newspapers or the theorists call the higher prices, "inflation." But the inflation is not the higher prices; the inflation is the new money pumped into the market. It is this new money that then inflates the prices. And the government asks, "What happened? How should one man know? How should I, the man in the department of finance, know that this additional money is really spent and that this spending must raise prices because the quantity of goods did not increase?" The government is very innocent. It doesn't know what happened, you know, because this happened in another department of the government.

And the governments try to find somebody who is responsible—but not the government. They consider the man who *asks* for higher prices responsible. But he *must* ask for higher prices because there are now more people wanting to buy his produce, you know. He has 100 units to sell each at 5 pieces of money. And now people are coming—not with 500 but with 600 pieces of money in their pockets—and the buyers must, therefore, in order to prevent other men from getting the things they want, pay higher prices. Now we have the inflation.

Years ago, many, many years ago—60 years ago—I wrote my first essay dealing with the problems of money. It was a study about the inflation in Austria and the way in which one day the government decided to abandon the inflation and to return to stable money in spite of the very heavy opposition of the party that was dedicated to the brilliant old system of inflation. I gave this essay to my teacher, Böhm-Bawerk, for publication in his economic magazine which he published with some friends. And one of his friends, a former Minister of Finance, Dr. Ernst von Plener, having read the manuscript, invited me to talk with him about the manuscript, about the problem. He was very interested in view of the fact that he was one of the Ministers of Finance dealt with in this essay. We had a very interesting conversation and at the end of this conversation, Dr. von Plener said, "It's a very interesting study that you have given to our magazine. But I am astonished that a young man like you is interested in a problem of the past like inflation. There was *really*, in the 19th century, in almost every country of the world, inflation. But it will *not* return. This will *never* come again. Can you imagine that the British Empire, Germany, France, the United States, will go off the gold standard? No! Impossible! And the fact that *these* countries will keep to the gold standard will force all the other nations also to remain with the gold standard."

I said, "I would like to be of your opinion. But as I look around in the literature about money and what is being written and published *every* day, also in the United States, also in England, and so on, about this problem, then I see, or I believe I see, a tendency toward a return to these problems of inflation." And I think I was right! Twenty years later, after the First World War, after all those things that had happened after the War, Dr. von Plener told me, "Remember our conversation. You were right and I was wrong. But your opinion would have been better advice for these countries." I admitted that without any difficulty. And I would have to admit it today again.

In the years after the First World War, American economists frequently visited Vienna and I had the pleasure of talking with them, and explaining inflation and conditions as they prevailed at that time in Austria and in other European countries. And, as you know, when people are talking about economic problems, they are talking and talking until finally it is late in the evening, very late in the evening. And so it was. Then I told them, "I will now give you an explanation as to why conditions in the country are not so satisfactory. I will take you for a little walk to the center of the city, past a definite building." This was at 11 o'clock or midnight. And we went. It was very quiet. But then they heard a noise, the sound of the printing machines that were printing banknotes day and night for the government. The result in Vienna was very modest you know; the American dollar which had been five Austrian crowns became 14,000 or 17,000 Austrian crowns. The inflation was bad, you are right. But this was a very modest inflation; the achievement of inflation in Germany was much greater you know. It took billions of marks you know to make one U.S. dollar. You consider this a joke, but it was a tragedy of course. For the people whose property it destroyed, it was a catastrophe.

Inflation today is probably the most important phenomenon in political life and political conditions. Fortunately there is still in this country, and I hope it will succeed one day, a very reasonable opposition against inflationary measures. But for many governments it is simply a question of being in a situation of needing more money and they think it is perfectly reasonable to increase the quantity of money. If we want to have a system of money that works and operates, one must not increase the quantity of money without realizing at every step that one is approaching a very dangerous point, the point at which the whole thing breaks down. You will say that this is something very general; what reference does it have to the problems of daily policies, monetary policies. It has a very important reference. The reference is that when you are operating with something that can be a deadly poison, not always but it can be, then you must be very careful. You must be very careful not to go to a certain point. This is something which one may also say about all the medicines that influence the nerves and minds of people. The doctor saves the lives of some people by giving them some chemical in a quantity which he precisely determines and knows. And if the quantity were increased up to a certain point, then the same chemical would be a deadly poison.

We have a similar situation with inflation. Where does inflation start? It starts as soon as you increase the quantity of money. And where does the danger point begin? That is another problem. The question cannot be answered precisely. People must realize that you cannot give a statesman advice: "This is the point up to which you may go and beyond this point you may not go, and so on, you know." Life is not as simple as that. But what we have to realize, what we have to know when we are dealing with money and monetary problems, is always the same. We have to realize that the increase in the quantity of money, the increase of those things which have the power to be used for monetary purposes, must be restricted at every point.

The real problem is that we have a quantity of money in most countries, including the United States, a quantity that is continually increasing. And the effect of this increase is that prices of commodities and services are going up and people are asking for higher wages. And the government says this is "an inflationary pressure." I see this word a hundred times everyday in the newspapers, but I don't know what "an inflationary pressure" is. There is no such thing as "an inflationary pressure." Nothing is inflationary except an increase in the quantity of money. Either there *is* an increase in the quantity of money, or there is *no* increase in the quantity of money.

There is a practical solution from the theoretical point of view—the gold standard. As long as we are using as a medium of exchange the precious metal gold, we have under present day conditions no special problems to deal with. But as soon as we are increasing the quantity of paper money, as soon as we say, "A little bit more, it doesn't matter, and so on," then we are entering a field in which the problems become very different. We can have today a rather satisfactory system of monetary payments when we accept the idea that gold can be used as a medium of exchange without any restrictions. But then we may say theoretically from the point of view of clear fine theories, this is not very satisfactory. Perhaps! But it is very satisfactory from the point of view of the operation of a monetary system and the market. And this is what counts.

CHAPTER SEVEN

Inflation Destroys Savings

Everything that is done by a government against the purchasing power of the monetary unit is, under present conditions, done against the middle classes and the working classes of the population. Only these people don't know it. And this is the tragedy. The tragedy is that the unions and all these people are supporting a policy that makes all their savings valueless. And this is the great danger of the whole situation.

The conditions under which people are living in the industrial countries of the west, which today means in practically all the countries where the standard of civilization has made some progress since the 16th or 17th century, the masses are in a position, fortunately, in the years in which they are able to work, in which they are in full health, to provide for the state of affairs as it will prevail in later years when they will either be absolutely unfit to work or when their capacity to work will have decreased on account of old age or other changes. Under conditions as they are today, these people can only provide for their old age practically by either entering into labor contracts which give them a pension for their later age, or they can save a part of their income and invest it in such a way that they can use it in later years. These investments can be either simple savings deposits with banks, or they can be life insurance policies or bonds, for instance, government bonds which appear in many countries as perfectly safe. In all these cases the future of these people who are providing in this way for their old age, for their families and children is closely connected with the purchasing power of the monetary unit.

The man who owns an agricultural estate, the producer of oil or of foods, or the businessman who owns a factory is in a different position.

When the prices of the products which he is selling go up on account of the inflation, he will not be hurt in the same way in which other people are hurt by the inflation. The owner of common stock will see that, by and large, most of this common stock is going up in price to the same degree as the prices of commodities are going up on account of the inflation. But it is different for people with fixed incomes. The man who retired 25 years ago with a yearly pension, let us say of $3,000, was by and large in a good situation or was believed to be in a good situation. But this was at a time when prices were much lower than they are today. I don't want to say any more about this situation and the consequences and effects of inflation for the people. What I want to point out is that the greatest problem today is precisely this, although the people don't realize it. The danger is due to the fact that people consider inflation as something which hurts *other* people. They realize very well that they too have to suffer because the prices of the commodities they are buying go up continually, but they don't realize fully that the greatest danger for them is precisely the progress of inflation and the effect it will have on the value of their savings.

All over Europe today you see unrest due to the fact that the European masses are discovering that they have been the losers in all these financial operations which their own governments have considered as a very wonderful thing. And, therefore, also from the point of view of making it possible for the masses to enjoy the improvement of economic conditions and to make them partners, real partners, in the great development of industrial production that is going on practically now already in all countries of Europe and North America, even including Mexico, it is necessary to abandon the policy of inflation. The great unrest that is today characteristic of everything that is going on in Europe, the revolutionary ideas of the masses, especially of the sons of the middle classes who are studying at the universities, are due to the fact that the European governments, with the exception perhaps of the government of the little country Switzerland and other such very small countries, have in the last sixty years again and again embarked upon a policy of limitless inflation.[1]

[1] Mises was referring to the student riots that took place in Paris in the spring of 1968. The British had devalued the pound on November 18, 1967 from US$2.80 to US$2.40 and there was an international gold crisis in March 1968. The French wanted to return to the gold standard. In May "rebellious students at the Sorbonne and elsewhere, rioted, battled police and were joined by some 10,000,000 workers who launched nationwide strikes and took over many factories. The nation was almost completely paralyzed." Finally after pay increases were awarded the strikers and Army tanks were called out, normalcy was returned in early June. See *World Almanac, 1969*, pp. 63, 72, 512–513. —BBG

When talking about conditions in France, one should not overlook what inflation actually means. The French were right when, in the nineteenth century and in the beginning of our century, they declared that the social stability and the welfare of France is to a great extent based upon the fact that the masses of the French population are owners of government-issued bonds and therefore consider the financial welfare of the country, of the government, as their *own* financial advantage. And now this has been destroyed. Frenchmen who were not in business themselves, i.e., the majority of the population, were fanatical savers. All their savings were destroyed when the tremendous inflation reduced the value of the franc to practically nothing. The French franc may not have declined completely to zero, but for a Frenchman, who had $100 before and then had only one dollar—for such a Frenchman, the difference was not very great. Only a very few people can still consider themselves owners of some property when their property is reduced to 1% of what it was before.

In talking about inflation, we should not forget that over and above the consequences of destroying a country's monetary standard, there is the danger that depriving the masses of their savings will make them desperate. For decades there were only a very few who would agree with me in this position. Even so, I was astonished to read today in *Newsweek* that the majority of the people in the nation are not interested in the preservation of the purchasing power of the monetary unit. Unhappily, the article did not say that the destruction of the savings of the masses was a much more serious matter than the "famous" war now being waged on poverty.

It is ridiculous for the government to finance a "war on poverty"[2] by taxing, inflating, and spending, and so sacrificing the savings of the masses who are trying to improve themselves through their own efforts. This is one of the many contradictions which we have in our political, not our economic, system. To explain what I have in mind, consider the dreadful contradiction of the American government when it says: "We have to wage a war against poverty. Certainly many people are poor and we must make them wealthier." And yet this government taxes the people in order to make bread more expensive. You will say, "So, bread is more expensive; this is an exception." But it is *not* an exception! The American govern-

[2] President Lyndon Johnson had announced, in his January 8, 1964 State of the Union address, an "unconditional war on poverty in America." The money was intended especially for "the chronically distressed areas of Appalachia." (*World Almanac, 1965*, p. 142) By December of that year, Congress had appropriated $784.2 millions for various projects in Appalachia and parts of 10 other states, primarily for highways and new jobs. (*World Almanac, 1965*, pp. 42, 47)

ment spends also billions of tax money in order to make cotton more expensive. Cotton goods are certainly not luxury goods; they are perhaps luxury goods when compared with bread, but the government does the same thing, it follows the same policy, with bread.

The *real* war on poverty was the "industrial revolution" and the industrialization of modern factories. At the beginning of the nineteenth century, shoes and stockings were luxury items for most of the people of continental Europe; they were not articles of daily wear. And the condition of these people was not improved by taxing, by taking money or shoes from the rich to give to the poor. It was the shoe industry, not the riches of the government, that improved the condition of the poor, that made a revolutionary change in the peoples' condition.

A statesman may say, "If I had more money to spend I could do things which would make me very popular in my country." The government tries to make itself popular by doing these things, but the technique it uses is to spend; and then it tries to ascribe to itself the good results of an expenditure. An expenditure is not always good. Sometimes an expenditure is just buying bombs and throwing them into a foreign country. But if the expenditure is beneficial, let us say if it makes it possible to improve some things in the country, then the statesman says, "Look, you never had such a wonderful life as you have under my regime. There are some bad people, some inflationists, some people who are profiteers, but I have nothing to do with them. This is not my fault." And so on.

Our economic situation depends largely on the relation of the government and the ruling political party or parties to the labor unions. We have "inflation," in the sense of higher prices, built into our economic system because the unions every year, every two years, or in exceptional cases every three years, ask for higher wages. The great majority of workers want continually higher wages and they assume wages can be manipulated *ad libitum*, at will, by the government. The unions have the power, by using violence, with the aid of certain laws and of certain institutions in Washington, to force people to agree to their wage demands. If wages do not continue to go up, no one knows what will happen. The only possible solution to the inflation problem is an open opposition to the unions and to the idea that higher money wages are the only means for improving the condition of the masses. Union members should also realize that their conditions would improve if the money prices of the things they wanted to buy went down, even if their money wages did not rise. I do not want to say anything more about this problem except to add that the government started it when it began to increase the quantity of money by printing it.

To give an example of how inflation destroys savings, there was in a European country a poor boy educated in an asylum for orphans, very well educated because when he had finished school and his life in the orphanage he emigrated to the United States. In the course of a long life he accumulated a considerable fortune by producing and selling something which was very successful. When he died, after living 45 years in the United States, he left a considerable fortune of $2,000,000. Not everybody leaves such a fortune; this was certainly exceptional. This man made a will according to which this $2,000,000 was to be sent back to Europe to establish another orphan asylum such as that in which this man had been educated. This was just before World War I. The money was sent back to Europe. According to the usual procedure it had to be invested in government bonds of this country, interest to be paid every year to keep up the asylum. But the war came, and the inflation. And the inflation reduced to zero this fortune of $2,000,000 invested in European Marks—simply to zero.

To give another example, a German who in 1914 owned a fortune which was the equivalent of US$100,000 had left from that fortune nine years later one-half cent perhaps, something like that, or five cents—it doesn't make any difference; he had lost everything.

And there were similar experiences in the European universities. For instance, lots of foundations were set up in the course of centuries by people who wanted to make it possible for poor boys to study at the university and to achieve what they had achieved from the good education they had gotten at these universities. And what happened? In all these countries, in Germany, France, Austria and Italy, there came great inflations. And these inflations again destroyed these investments. For whose benefit? For the benefit, of course, of the government. And what did the government do with the money? It spent it; it threw it away.

People still believe, however, that destroying the value of the monetary unit is something that does not hurt the masses. But it *does* hurt the masses. And it hurts them first. There is no better way to bring about a tremendous revolution than to destroy the savings of the masses which are invested in savings deposits, insurance policies, and so on. An example of what I mean was furnished by the president of a bank in Vienna. He told me that as a young man in his twenties he had taken out a life insurance policy much too large for his economic condition at the time. He expected that when it was paid out it would make him a well-to-do burgher.

But when he reached his sixtieth birthday, the policy became due. The insurance, which had been a tremendous sum when he had taken it out thirty five years before, was just sufficient to pay for the taxi ride back to his office after going to collect the insurance in person. Now what had happened? Prices went up, yet the monetary quantity of the policy remained the same. He had in fact for many, many decades made savings. For whom? For the government to spend and devastate.

If you talk about a catastrophe of the money, you need not always have in mind a total breakdown of the currency system. Such a thing did occur in this country in 1781 with the so-called "Continental Currency." And it occurred in many other countries later, for instance, the most famous inflation, the breakdown of the German mark currency in 1923. These changes are not the same, nor to the same degree in various countries. But one should not exaggerate the difference in the effects brought about by the greater inflations as against the smaller inflations. The effects of the "smaller inflations" are also bad.

We must realize that in the market economy, in the capitalistic system, all inter-human relations that are not simply personal and intimate, all interpersonal relations, are expressed, made, counted in money terms. A change in the purchasing power of money affects everybody and not in such a way that you can say it is beneficial if the purchasing power of the money is going up or down. All our relationships, the relations between individuals and the state, and between individuals and other individuals, are based on money. And this is true not only for the capitalistic countries. It is true for all kinds of conditions. For instance, in predominantly agricultural countries in which the small- or medium-sized farm prevails, it is usual, necessarily usual, that at the death of the owner of such a farm, one of his children takes over the farm and the other children, the brothers and sisters inherit only a part of the farm. The man who gets the farm has to pay to the others in the course of his life, step-by-step, the share of the inheritance which is theirs. That means that the man who inherits the farm gets no more and no less than the other members of the family. But when this is arranged by transferring the property to one heir and giving the others claims in money terms against this heir, claims to be settled in the course of the years, this means that everyday, if there is an inflation in progress, the share of the man who got the farm is increasing and the shares of the other brothers and sisters are sinking.

We have had in this country, continually now for several years, an outspoken inflationary increase in the quantity of circulating money. However, conditions are influenced by this situation. There has been a general rise in prices. You hear about it; you read about it; people compare prices and talk about it enough. Yet I shouldn't exaggerate what has happened already to the dollar. What has happened to the dollar is still not something that makes a catastrophe unavoidable. If you were to go to certain other countries—Brazil or Argentina, for instance—you would be in a country which also has inflation, but a much bigger inflation. And if you ask a man in Brazil what he considers a stable money which does not drop in purchasing power, he would say, "The U.S. dollar … that's wonderful!" Of course, when compared with his country's money.

The problem of money, the practical problem of money today in the whole world is precisely this: The governments believe that in the situation which I have pointed out before, when there is a choice between an unpopular tax and a very popular expenditure, there is a way out for them—the way toward inflation. This illustrates the problem of going away from the gold standard.

Money is the most important factor in a market economy. Money was created by the market economy, not by the government. It was a product of the fact that people substituted step-by-step a common medium of exchange for direct exchange. If the government destroys the money, it not only destroys something of extreme importance for the system, the savings people have set aside to invest and to take care of themselves in some emergency; it also destroys the very system itself. Monetary policy is the center of economic policy. So all the talk about improving conditions, about making people prosperous by credit expansion, by inflation, is futile!

CHAPTER
EIGHT

Inflation and Government Controls

Human cooperation can be organized according to two different models. One is the model of absolute rule by one ruler only, the socialist model—everything is organized under the leadership of a leader, *der Führer.* The term is not very much used in the Anglo-Saxon language because people did not think of it as a system that can really work. But in the countries in which socialism prevails the term, *der Führer*, the leader, is very well known. In those countries everything depends upon this autocratic regime; everybody has to obey the orders issued from one central authority. People who like the system call it "order;" people who don't like it call it "slavery."

This system in which people must obey the orders issued from a central authority is very well known to anybody who has served in an army. For the army, it is the only possible system. If one criticizes the centralized system, we must not forget that it is suitable only for a special purpose, for the special end which it can attain.

The characteristic of the market is that government does not issue orders that the people must obey; it does not control prices; prices and wages are determined by demand and supply on the market. This system is the system that brought about the constitutions and all those commodities and services which together can be called modern civilized life. The opposite of the market is the abolition of the market and its substitution by the socialist or communist state. That means planning, central planning, where everything is determined by decrees and orders of the government.

Government officials cannot ignore public opinion; they cannot ignore the ideas and practices of the people. The government is never in a position to make any laws it wants. It cannot afford to take into consideration only the views of the people who are running the government. So laws tend to follow accepted practices and theories. And that is true in the field of money too. With respect to money, government must accept and acknowledge the money that has evolved out of the actions and ideas of individuals.

Let us take the following political situation. The government wants to spend more than it has spent up to yesterday, but it doesn't have the money. And it doesn't want to tax more, or for political reasons it simply cannot tax more. Nor can it borrow the money, because from their point of view conditions for borrowing appear unsatisfactory. The government wants to spend more and doesn't want to tax the people. The government wants to appear as Santa Claus, which is a very agreeable situation, a more popular situation than that of a tax collector. Therefore, the government does not tax the people to get the money for its new expenditure; it inflates; it prints the money. The important point to remember regarding inflation is that, while the money in circulation is increased, other things remain unchanged. This inflation is very cheap, you know; it is a very cheap procedure. What happens then? Prices go up. The government, of course, wants a way out, a solution, so it is apt to try price-fixing. The government fails to recognize the fact that if the public really obeys its price-fixing orders, sellers will sell their entire supply of commodities to regular customers at the former or fixed prices with the result that those into whose pockets the additional money goes will find nothing to buy.

I want to give a typical example of how government price controls work. In the First World War and again in the Second, the German government and the English, among others, embarked upon inflation as a means of financing the war. The addition of new money to that already in circulation brought about an up-trend in prices which the government did not like. The government wanted business as usual. But it was obviously not business as usual. Therefore, the German government, as well as others, resorted to price controls.

Now, if prices are fixed below what they would have been in the unhampered market, high cost producers are bound to suffer losses. The government starts, let us say, by fixing the price of milk. As a result, the higher-cost producers cease bringing milk to the market and convert their milk into other end products, butter, for example. Thus, the quantity of milk on the market not only does not increase, but actually decreases, precisely the opposite of what the government wanted. The government wanted milk to be more readily available to the average family, but the quantity of milk decreases. When the government approaches the producers for an explanation, their answer is that they would have suffered losses in producing milk because of the price they had to pay, let us say for fodder, and, therefore, they turned their milk production into butter for which there was no fixed maximum price. The government then price-fixes fodder. And then the same story is repeated with fodder. Thus, the government continues step-by-step until it reaches what the Germans in the First World War referred to as the "Hindenburg Plan," a complete socialization of everything.

The German government broke down at the end of the War. But several years later the Brüning government reinstated price controls which Hitler carried to their final conclusion. Price controls transformed private ownership and private production into a system of complete government control of everything. German communism, national socialism, under Hitler did not legally expropriate the owners of the means of production, but every economic step was determined by government. There were still entrepreneurs, although the name "entrepreneurs" was eliminated; they were called "shop managers." They were at the head of business organizations, but they had to comply completely and exactly with the government orders. They had to buy raw materials at prices set by government, sell to other firms at prices determined by government, and employ workers assigned to them by government.

There is no third economic system which makes it possible on the one hand to have a free market and on the other hand to avoid socialism or communism. Interference with the market inevitably brings about effects which, from the point of view of the interfering authorities, are even worse than the state of affairs they wanted to alter. In order to make the system work the authorities go farther step-by-step until they bring about a situation under which the initiative of everybody else is destroyed, and everything depends on the authorities, upon the leadership of government.

The reason we do not have price controls here today is because of the experiences in other countries. Again and again the government repeats that we need to control prices. Yet it does not tell the cigarette manufacturers that it is *forbidden* for them to raise the price of a pack by one cent. Instead the government tries to talk with the cigarette manufacturers and with the representatives of a thousand other firms so as to pressure them. While the government has not as yet embarked on price control it hasn't really done anything to prevent the present system from operating in a way it does not like. As a matter of fact, quite the contrary. It has built inflation into our present system—inflation even in the popularly-accepted meaning in which the government uses the term, that is higher prices.

We see, therefore, that the problem of money is much more than only the problem of the organization of the market. The market is today fighting for its independence and existence. The government tries to interfere with the market and we are now just one day, one year, nobody knows how far away from what is called control of prices. And that means the abolition of the market.

CHAPTER
NINE

Money, Inflation, and War

Now, one may say that there are situations when the government is forced to increase the quantity of money, when it is the highest wisdom on the part of the government to proceed in this way. Such a situation would be when the country is menaced by invasion by foreign armies. What can the government do then? It must spend more. And as the people are not paying enough in taxes and the government can't tax them any more because they don't have more money, the government has to print money. To see if this reasoning is correct, let us now talk about historical problems.

What does this mean that there are some situations in which you cannot avoid inflating? One talks about one particular case—war! Now, please! In a war governments needs armaments and various other things in order to defend the country—I don't want to enumerate them. All these things must be produced and they cost money. If the citizens are not prepared to supply the armaments or to give the money to pay for the armaments, then their country will be defeated in the war, and the country will become dependent. But an increase in the quantity of paper money does not change this.

There can be certain conditions under which the government inflated and you can say the situation was such that the alternative to inflation, to increasing the quantity of money, was also very bad. When the American colonies were fighting against England in the War of Independence, they proceeded to inflation. The alternative, let us assume, would have been defeat, because certainly in the eyes of the men responsible for this inflation, for this increase in the quantity of money, this was the alternative. You can say that, if it was really possible to preserve the independence of what later became the United States through inflation, then the inflation was justified. The catastrophe couldn't be avoided then. But the catastrophe, the breakdown of this currency in 1781 after the Revolutionary War, did not mean the same thing that it would have meant years later when the economic conditions changed. In the years of the Revolutionary War the American colonies were a predominantly agricultural country; most of the people were owners or workers of an agricultural piece of land and could survive the catastrophe which the breakdown of the American currency, the Continental Currency, meant after the Revolutionary War. Getting food was not then a matter of going to the market. They didn't use money to buy food or hardly any other things. When the Continental government inflated in 1781, the man who had a small farm and who worked with his family on this farm and had a few dollars, he lost these few dollars because of the inflation, but that didn't affect him very much. Therefore, the whole problem of inflation was only of minor importance for the Americans at the end of the Revolutionary War.

We cannot compare conditions today in the United States with those in the United States of 1781. Today we no longer have the simple system which existed at that time under which the money economy meant very little for most people. We have had other such examples in the past. But under the conditions of a highly developed society, under the division of labor under the conditions of society in which practically everybody depends on working for other people and is paid by money and uses this money in order to buy things, under these conditions which I do not have to describe because they are known to everybody, a breakdown of the currency would mean something quite different. There is no excuse for a government that resorts to inflation today saying, "But, don't forget, we have an old tradition of inflation. We are an independent nation today because we had an inflation in the War of Independence, in the Revolution." You cannot compare conditions.

There was also, for instance, the great problem of the United States, the greatest historical problem for the United States, the Civil War in the 1860s. There were the Northern States and the Southern States. And the Southern States were in a very bad situation because they had very little industry. Their agricultural production was great, but their industries were not in a position to produce the needed armaments. From the first day of the Civil War, this was a very unfortunate situation for the Southerners especially as the Navy of the North was in a position to prevent trade between the Southern States and the European countries which would have been in a position to deliver armaments to the South. Now it is impossible to improve a country's military situation by inflation, even in a country in which all the materials required for the war are available. Therefore, even from the point of view of the necessities of a situation in which a country is fighting for its survival, inflation *as such* is not a measure to improve conditions. Now the shortage of armaments could be affected in no way by the fact that the secession government increased the quantity of money. But if you were a statesman in the Southern States and you were already approaching defeat, and somebody asked you, "Don't you know that printing money, banknotes, more and more dollar bills of the southern quality, will destroy this system?" this southern statesman would have answered, "Why are you talking about the money? The problem now is whether the Southern States, our system, which is more important than anything else in the world, should survive or not. Our war, or our rebellion," it depends on how you looked upon this problem, "is finished." He could print money to try to get what was needed to keep on fighting. And so he printed the notes, and more and more notes. And they went to zero.

With the outbreak of World War I, many governments that had not resorted to inflation previously and had provided all the money they needed by taxation, started printing additional banknotes, paper notes. The effect necessarily was an upward movement of prices. The governments were probably not so naive that they did not know what their new methods of providing money for the government spending would bring about. The governments knew that the policy of adding enormous quantities of new additional money into the market would necessarily bring about a tendency toward higher prices. But what did the government do? With the outbreak of the war, with the change in their policies, they also began making laws which punished people who, according to the ideas of the government, were asking higher prices for commodities than they had asked before. What the governments of some countries, of many countries, did in this regard is just unbelievable—I would say it was a "swindle"—they introduced a new crime, a new method of punishing citizens. They declared that there was a special crime of profiteering. And they began to imprison people. Why? Because, these governments said, these people were profiteers; they were asking more than they had before, more than the government thought necessary.

I don't want to say that inflation is a vice and call it "immoral." I don't care for this method of criticizing inflation. But seriously, there is one thing about inflation that we can know for sure. You cannot tell today whether or not people in the government tomorrow or the day after tomorrow will not choose for some reason to increase the quantity of money, that is to inflate. They may have an excuse. They will say: "Inflation is bad. There should never be any question of inflation." And then they will add: "Yes, but we didn't take into account the conditions of an important war. Really this situation didn't exist before." And then they will increase the quantity of money.

In one of the many belligerent countries of the last fifty years, there was one Minister of Finance who, when asked "Why do you inflate? Is it not a crime that you are destroying the currency of your country by issuing more money and therefore raising prices?" answered, "In time of war, it is the duty of every citizen of every branch of the government and of every part of the country to contribute as much as possible to the defense of the country. From this point of view, as Minister of Finance, I contributed by printing money."

The Germans before the first World War were highly intelligent and very patriotic. But unfortunately for decades and decades the government and all the professors it had appointed to the universities had taught very bad economics, especially monetary economics. Sixty years ago, a German professor, a teacher of economics of great renown, G. F. Knapp, declared: "Money is what the government says it is. Money is a government product. The government is sovereign and free to do what it wants." He was not saying something new. The only new thing was that a professor was saying it, that all the people in the government said, "All right," and that even those who did not say "all right" acted as it they considered it all right. That meant that the governments claimed the privilege to declare what people had in their minds when they made agreements concerning money. It was not remarkable that the professor said this, you know—professors sometimes say things that are not remarkable. But what was very remarkable was that the people accepted it.

An American economist, B. M. Anderson, predicted Professor Knapp's influence would be such that students would probably "have to read his book if they wished to understand the next decade of German history.... Look at your German theory, look at the German so-called economic doctrine on money and then you will see what will happen to the German money."[1] And he was perfectly right! The result came very soon. When

[1] "[T]here is a fair chance that American students may have to read his book [G. F. Knapp, *Staatliche Theorie des Geldes*, Leipzig, 1905] if they wish to understand the next

Germany went to war, the government didn't realize, and still less did the people realize, that what one needs to fight the war is not paper money but arms and various other things. So they printed paper money. And they printed paper money day and night. The result was that the German paper money from pre-World War I deteriorated in value. The parity with the American dollar in 1914 expressed in German marks was 4.2 as it had been for 60, 80, and 100 years before. You know what the cost of a postage stamp is. The German monetary policy of increasing the quantity of money, printing it continually, until a German postage stamp in the early 20's of our century cost several million marks. Imagine the situation that developed in 1923 when someone who bought a stamp in order to mail a letter to the next village had to pay several hundred million marks. Twenty million marks was more than the wealth of the richest people in Germany in the earlier period. At the end of this inflation, nine years later, the dollar was 4.2 *billion* marks, something which is purely fantastic because there are no people who have an idea, a living idea, of what a billion is. This was the outcome of the economic doctrine that money was a creation of the government. The fact that the government had printed money, that the government had increased the quantity of money, did not improve the situation of the German armed forces or the German resistance. It was simply an attempt to deceive the people in Germany and outside of Germany about the effects of the war.

It is true that the Reichsbank printed more and more paper money. *But the significance of this famous German inflation of 1923 consisted in the fact that these pieces of paper had legal tender value.* Now what did this mean? The government assumed the right to say, not only what money was, but also to decree what people were bound to accept as money. Legal tender legislation makes it impossible for anybody to refuse to accept the paper money. In the same way, the American dollar inflation today [1969] consists of the fact that the paper dollar has legal tender value and at the same time that gold holding is made illegal. Holdings of gold were confiscated and it has been made illegal to deal with gold.[2]

decade of German monetary history. It will be well for Germany if this is not the case!" B. M. Anderson, *The Value of Money*. New York: Macmillan, 1917. p. 435*n*. —**BBG**

[2] U.S. citizens regained the right to own gold only after Mises died in 1973. Legislation effective December 31, 1974, permitted gold sales to resume in January 1975. —**BBG**

CHAPTER
TEN

The Constitutional Side of Inflation

When we talk about these things we must not forget that they do not have only an economic side; they also have a constitutional side. You may say that government is the most important institution. The government *is* very important in many regards. Perhaps one overrates the importance of the government, but one does *not* overrate the importance of *good* government.

Modern constitutions, the political systems of all nations that are not ruled by barbarian despots, are based upon the fact that the government depends financially upon the people, indirectly upon the men that the voters have elected for the constitutional assembly. And this system means that the government has no power to spend anything that has not been given it by the people, through the constitutional procedures which make it possible for the government to collect taxes. This is the fundamental political institution. And it is a fundamental political problem if the government can inflate. If the government has the power to print its own money, then this constitutional procedure becomes absolutely useless.

Our whole political system is based upon the fact that the voters are sovereign, that the voters are electing Congress and other such institutions in the various states that rule the country. We call the United States a democracy because the rule of the country is in the hands of the voters. The voters determine everything. And this distinguishes the system, not only from the despotic systems of other countries, but also from the conditions as they prevailed in earlier days, in countries that already had parliamentary institutions and parliamentary government, at that time. However, there has developed, especially in the last decade, a problem of constitutional law, that is whether the government must get the approval of the people through Congress when it wants to spend, or whether the government, because it is established and has at its disposal a number of armed men, is free to spend as it wishes, simply by increasing the quantity of money. People must realize that the question is "Who should be supreme? The parliaments elected by the voters, who can restrict government spending by refusing to grant the power to tax? Or institutions that want to override the interests of the people by increasing the quantity of money to expand government spending and so do away with the prerogative and independence of the individual voter?"

If we do not succeed in restoring the monetary system that makes the individual independent to some extent of the interference of government institutions, government banks, government monetary authorities, government price ceilings, and so on, we will lose all the achievements of the free market and of the free initiative of the individuals, whatever methods of constitutional law we follow. If the government can inflate whenever it wants to spend, it can take away from the people without their agreement everything, their purchasing power, their savings, and so on. From this point of view there disappears even the fundamental principle which everybody sees as the difference between a Communist government and a government based on the idea of individual freedom, the preservation of free markets and the ability of the people to control the government.

If you look at the constitutional history of England in the 17th century, you learn that the Stuarts had problems with the British Parliament. The conflict consisted precisely in the fact that the Parliament was not prepared to give to the King of England the money he needed for purposes of which the Parliament didn't approve. The people disapproved of a great part of the government expenditures and Parliament was not anxious to impose taxes. The Stuart kings wanted to spend more than Parliament was prepared to give them. If the King at that time, in 1630 let us say, had asked one of those who are considered experts today in government finance, "What can I do? I don't have the money!" the "expert" would have said, "Unfortunately, your family, the Stuarts, came too early to their position as rulers. Two hundred years, three hundred years later, it would be much easier for such a government as you want to rule the country. A printing press would have been sufficient to make it possible for your government to spend all the money it needed to have an army and the other things needed to protect the King against the people." But the poor Stuarts were living in an age in which the technique of producing paper money had not been developed to a considerable extent. Charles I couldn't inflate, you know. There was no solution for him; he could not engage in deficit spending. This was the undoing of the Stuart family and the Stuart regime. And in the conflict which originated out of this, one member of the Stuart family lost his life in a very disagreeable way—Charles I lost his head.[1] And the Stuart family as such lost the crown of England. What the poor Stuarts didn't have was the facility of the printing press as it exists today.

The monetary problem we have to struggle with today is the problem of paying for government expenditures which are not accepted or, let us say, not approved, by the people. The conduct of government affairs, public affairs, is not different from the conduct of the financial and monetary conduct of private affairs. If the government wants to spend, it has to collect the money; it must tax the people. If it doesn't tax, but increases the quantity of money in order to spend more, then it brings about an inflation. The difference between the conditions in 18th century England and the conditions in other countries, let us say for instance in Russia, consisted of the fact that the Russian government was free to take away from its subjects what it wanted while the British government was not. The British government had to comply with the provisions of a set of laws that limited the amount of money the government had the right to collect from its citizens. And it had to spend this money precisely according to the wishes of the people.

All our constitutional laws and our system of government are based upon the fact the government is not permitted to do anything that violates this system of laws representing the moral and actual ideas and philosophies of our people. But if the government is in a position to increase the quantity of money, all these provisions become absolutely meaningless and useless. If it is said that the government has to spend, is entitled to spend, a definite amount of money for keeping people in prisons, this means something. There is a definite reason for its spending. All our legal provisions are influenced to some extent by the fact that this is the amount of money which is given to the government for this purpose. But if the government is in a position to increase the quantity of money to use for its own purposes, then all these things become merely a theoretical expression of something which has practically no meaning at all. We must not forget that all the protection given to individuals through constitutions and laws disappears if the government is in a position to destroy the meaning of ev-

[1] Charles I was beheaded on January 30, 1649

ery inter-human relation by undermining the system of indirect exchange and money which is called the market. And this is much more important than any other problems we talk about today. It is the interference of the government with violence that has spoiled money, that has destroyed money in the past, and that is perhaps destroying it again today.

Some years ago you could frequently read quotations saying that Lenin said that the best method to destroy the free enterprise system would be to destroy the monetary system. Now a professor in Germany has demonstrated that Lenin never said this. But if Lenin *had* said this, it would have been the only correct thing that he ever said.

The monetary problem which we have in this country, which you have in every country today, is the same—to keep the budget in equilibrium, to balance income and outgo, revenue and expenditure without printing an additional quantity of banknotes, without increasing the quantity of the monetary units. This is not only a problem of economics. It is also the fundamental problem of constitutional government, you know. Constitutional government is based upon the fact that the government can only spend what it has collected in taxes. And it can only tax the people if the people accept it by the vote of their representatives in parliament. And in this way the voters are the sovereigns. The problem of monetary management in a modern country cannot, therefore, be separated from the constitutional problem, from the doctrine that says that all problems of government, all governmental matters are decided ultimately by the vote of the people. Whether you call this democracy or popular government doesn't make any difference. But there is no monetary or budgetary problem that can be separated from the constitutional problem of who rules the country, who determines ultimately what has to be done in the country.

CHAPTER ELEVEN

Capitalism, the Rich and the Poor

It is a very popular assumption, criticized only very rarely by people, that the capitalistic system brings about satisfactory conditions for a minority of profiteers, while the masses become more and more impoverished. Of all the enormous problems connected with the monetary crisis, I want to deal with this problem especially because the most popular, or one of the most popular, ideas of Marxism is that the system of capitalism brings about the progressive impoverishment, the progressive deterioration of the economic state of affairs of the masses, for the benefit of a shrinking number of people who become richer and richer from year to year.

People believe that what is going on with these monetary problems today concern the well-to-do and that simple people are not so much interested. I want to show you how erroneous this idea is. It is thought that when the government inflates and as a result lowers the purchasing power of the monetary unit, this is of advantage to the masses, to the great majority of the people, and that only the rich are suffering. If you don't want to use the term "suffer," let us say have to pay higher prices for things. Now this idea, that the interested people are not the masses, not the majority of the people, but only the wealthy people and that it is only the wealthier and richer people that are concerned, is based on an ancient doctrine.

This doctrine was perfectly correct in the days of Solon (c. 638–559 BC) of Athens, or in the days of ancient Rome, of the Gracchi brothers (d. 121 and 133 BC), or in the Middle Ages. In the pre-capitalistic ages the rich people owned land and were, therefore, wealthy. They could save, increase their possessions by investing in real property, houses, businesses, landed property. Or they could increase their fortunes by dealing in a more conservative way with the forests which they owned. On the other hand there were people who were poor, very poor, people who had nothing, who might occasionally earn a small piece of money but who really had no opportunity to accumulate anything to improve their conditions. Under ancient conditions, the masses had no opportunity to save; the poor man had only the possibility of earning a few coins perhaps and of hiding these coins somewhere, perhaps in a dark corner of their premises, but this was all. He would always be under the temptation to spend them. Or he could lose them. Or somebody could steal them. The poor were not in a position to make their savings grow by lending them against interest. Even in England, the most advanced capitalistic country in the eighteenth century, it was not possible, for a poor man to save except by hoarding a few coins in an old stocking hidden somewhere in his house. Such savings bore no interest. Only the rich could invest money at interest, perhaps in mortgages, and so on.

At that time when people talked about creditors and debtors, they had in mind a state of affairs in which the wealthier a man was the more of a creditor he was, and the poorer a man was the more of a debtor he was. The whole idea was based on the assumption that the government ought to help the poor people who have heavy debts, while the rich who have claims are rich enough. Therefore, the method by which the government lowers the purchasing power of the monetary unit helps the debtors, because their debts are shrinking, and at the same time it goes against the creditors because their claims also are shrinking.

We are inclined to think that the situation today is similar, that the rich people today are creditors, certainly that they have no debts and are not debtors. But we no longer live under the conditions in which the authors dealt with these problems in the pre-capitalistic ages. The situation is very different today. It is very different because we have a very different organization of business, of business claims, and of the adjustment of business to the various individuals. Capitalism has enriched the masses, not all of them, of course, because capitalism has still to fight the hostility of the governments. But under capitalistic conditions it is no longer true that the creditors are the rich and the debtors are the poor. Capitalism has developed a great system making it possible for the masses of the poorest strata of the population, the people who have less—I don't want to say that they are poor in the sense in which one uses the term, only that they are poorer, less wealthy, than the rich people, than the entrepreneurs, and so on—to save and to invest their savings indirectly in the operation of business. The rich people are owners, for instance, of the common stock of a corporation. But the corporations owe money, either because they have issued bonds, corporate bonds, or because they have some current connection with a bank, employing money lent to them by the banks in the conduct of their affairs. Thus the great millionaires, the owners of real estate, the owners of common stock, and so on, are in this regard debtors. The masses, the people whom we call less wealthy than the richer people, have invested their savings in savings deposits, in bonds, in insurance policies, and so on. And the banks have money from the savings accounts of simple citizens who, therefore, are creditors. And if you do something, as practically all the governments do, against the purchasing power of the monetary unit today under present conditions, you are hurting *not* the rich, but the middle classes and the masses of people who are saving all their lives in order to enjoy a better old age and in order to make it possible for them to educate their children and so on.

The fact that government bonds are to some extent tax free means the government gives special privileges to the rich in order to attract them to the market for government bonds and so to become creditors. It is a very complicated system; one could call the system simply privileges in the way of lower taxes in order to make the wealthier strata of the population also interested in buying government bonds and in this way to make it possible for the government to spend more. But by and large we have to say that the great, the much greater part, of the privileges, of the "benefits"—"benefits" in quotations marks—which the people derive from the government's inflationary policy does not go to the masses but to those who are better off. And so the "benefits" of the inflation are *paid* for by the masses.

Not so long ago, there was the very powerful Nazi movement in Germany. Whatever you may say about Germany, you cannot say that it was an illiterate country. You couldn't say that the population of Germany was inexperienced in problems of capitalism and modern industrialism. In that country, Germany, one of the main slogans, a very popular slogan which brought millions of votes to the Nazi Party was: "Do away with interest slavery. You are slaves in paying interest to the rich people and we shall do away with interest slavery." Now what was this "interest slavery"? This was a fantastic idea, you know, for it was really to the masses, the poorer people, to whom the big corporations and other such institutions made interest payments. Yet practically nobody objected to this slogan. One eminent German newspaper, perhaps the best informed German newspaper with regard to economic problems, the *FRANKFURTER ZEITUNG*, published an article in which it said: "You people who accept this program of the Nazi Party of doing away with interest slavery, *do you know that you are creditors and not debtors?*" And they were, but they didn't know it. On the day when the *FRANKFURTER ZEITUNG* published this article on its first page, I was on the way to London traveling in the express train from one end of Germany to the other, from the Austrian frontier of Germany to the Dutch frontier. I could observe people reading this article and I told myself, "They don't understand these things, and so they are *bound* to suffer the consequences." And did they suffer the consequences? Of course! The mark became zero. This meant that all the assets, all the savings of the people, the creditors, disappeared, to the benefit of the debtors.

People in a country like the United States are saving in the years when they are in full vigor and can earn money. They are saving not only to meet unexpected conditions which could develop one day; they are saving systematically to enjoy income without working any longer in their old age. For instance, people are taking out life insurance policies; they are accumulating savings deposits; and they are making agreements with their employers according to which their employers are bound to pay them definite amounts as pension rights later; and so on. Now when there is an inflation going on, all these people are suffering, suffering because they are continually losing with the progress of inflation, because the progress of inflation means that the purchasing power of the monetary unit decreases. If we want to have a system in which the individual can plan for his own life and for the life of his family, if we want to have a system in which people can say: "If I have the opportunity to work and to save I will improve my own conditions and the conditions of my family." Then you must have a regular system of what one used to call "bourgeois security." But if the governments destroy the savings of their citizens again and again by inflating they bring about a situation in which the people do what these people in various European communist countries did and in which you hear again and again of violence and actions of destruction.

The example of Germany may help you realize that there are still many things to be learned about economic problems by everybody, not only by the managers of big banks, professional editors of journals of business, and so on. It is for this reason that I think everybody should be interested in these problems, *not* because they are more important than other things, nor on account of the fact that one should increase one's theoretical knowledge, but on account of the fact that one should know, in one's capacity as a voter and as a citizen, how to cooperate in the formation of one's own country, nation and the whole world's economic system. This is one of the reasons why one ought to deal with these problems. They are not very interesting to many people; they are not easy to study; but there is some reason to say they are fundamental for the preservation of one's own economic safety. We have to change the opinion of the people who believe that the monetary problem is something that concerns only groups of business, small groups of people, and so on.

CHAPTER
TWELVE

Currency Debasement in Olden Times

There is a very bad tendency for some historians to ascribe virtues to past generations and vices to those living today. I should be very unhappy if you were to believe that what I wanted to say was that all ages were very virtuous and that inflation appeared only since the invention of the printing press and the development of paper money. But there were inflationists already in the ages long, long before the printing press. You should not believe that inflation is a vice of our ages only. But the early governments had a more difficult problem than modern governments; the old governments had to deal with money manufactured, minted, out of the precious metals of silver or gold. And neither silver nor gold can be increased in quantity the way paper can be increased and stamped as money.

Again and again problems developed due to the fact that these pieces, these money pieces, were treated in a way that violated agreements and hurt the interest of some people for the benefit of others. If you want to study this process today, go to a museum where they have coins minted in the past and see what happened to the silver coins of the ancient Roman Empire of the third century. In a city like New York especially you have a great choice of such collections. You can look at these coins from various points of view. Most people look at them from the point of view of esthetics, but you could also look at them from the point of view of the history, not of coins, but of money. And there you will see what governments did in order to profit by falsifying the system of money, by increasing illegally and against the wishes of the people, the quantity of money.

The various kinds of money often had to fight two diseases. One disease, coin clipping, brought about a shrinking in the size and weight of the money pieces. And the second disease, which was very often connected with the first, changed the color of the silver coins, practically the only coins that were used in those days. What these old governments very often did was mint the coins in the traditional shape, but they mixed with the silver or gold some less precious metal like copper. Unfortunately copper has another color from silver, and another specific weight, so it could be discovered by people who had available the technological methods and instruments. It was a very difficult process. But they did this. And they didn't mention it. The coins slowly changed color in the course of the years, became a little bit reddish, not because they were affected by communist political ideas, which we today call "red," but because the governments that manufactured them put more and more copper in the coins which were assumed to contain only pure silver. When the governments became more and more aggressive, let us say, and added more and more copper, the color of the coins changed still more. Also most people are not color blind, especially not color blind in regard to money. This was too much for the people. So it was not very easy to continue to maintain this fiction. The coins became redder, and thinner and thinner.

The government maintained that the new coins minted by them were not different from the coins that had been minted before. In some way or other it was always a catastrophe for the citizens who did not know how to fight it. But it was a small evil, in spite of the fact that the effects, the unavoidable effects of inflation, became visible even in those days. It took some time for the simple citizens to discover it. But even citizens with very little information and knowledge of metal could discover the differences between a legally and ritually [properly] coined piece of money and another piece which was not. The people soon discovered that the government could spend more, and did spend more, than it had before. And prices went up.

The very famous Roman emperor, Diocletianus (286–305 AD), was very well known in religious history—I wouldn't say for his good deeds—but he was also known in the history of monetary annals. The more the silver content of the currency dropped as against the copper content, the more prices went up. And Diocletianus behaved in the same way as does our present government. He said it was somebody else's fault, the fault of the businessman. And therefore he resorted to price ceilings. Our price ceilings are printed on paper, but in the 3rd century, in the time of the emperor Diocletianus, such a system of price ceilings was printed on stone, the way we make our monuments. Therefore, his interference with the market has been preserved because of his law of prices. We still have carved on stone today the Law of Diocletianus in which he decreed price ceilings, maximum price ceilings, with the same success—or let us say with the same lack of success—with which our present day price ceilings meet.

The government's coining power, minting power, began simply with the fact that government said, "This is a definite quantity, a definite weight, and a definite quality of the precious metal." Previous to this, under the old Roman law, the original Roman law, the act of purchasing land required the presence of a man with scales to establish the correct weight of the quantity of precious metals entering into the transaction. At the end of this development, the government presumed that it had the right to say what the precious metal is and what a definite quantity of this precious metal is. An evolution of thousands of years—*really* thousands of years because there were such problems under special conditions 2,000 years ago—means that governments even then tried to interfere with the market by interfering with the money.

CHAPTER

THIRTEEN

Many Economics Professors Believe the Quantity of Money Should be Increased

Many famous professors of economics think that the supply of money is insufficient. It's unbelievable but we have now already for a long time, for many years, textbooks that say, in every new edition, that the quantity of money must increase by 2%, or 5%, or 7%. They change it from year to year—this is without any importance, what quantity they recommend is not so important—what is important is that they say that such an increase is good from the point of view of their policies. Wonderful! The government, the banks, can distribute more money, but they cannot distribute more *goods*. And this is the problem. As this additional money will raise the prices of goods, those who do not get any of this additional money are hurt. And this is what people don't realize, what they don't see. If this money is increased every year it means only that other groups can say "Why did *we* not get more?" And then the government gives them a quantity too and then again to others also. And this is the situation we have today. The question will always be: To whom do you give this additional quantity? Because if the additional quantity is given to somebody else, *your* conditions will be impaired.

I don't say that the quantity of money should be increased, or that it should be decreased. It is nonsensical if people complain in their textbooks about the increase in wealth of some groups of the population and about the decrease in wealth of other groups of the population and then recommend policies which will bring about precisely those conditions they consider wrong. From the point of view of most people, of the masses, an increase in the money supply is bad.

However, these inflationary methods are very popular. They are popular because they are very comfortable for the government. They are also very comfortable from the point of view of the individual member of a parliamentary body. The member of Parliament is not made responsible for higher taxes, but he accepts with pleasure the responsibility for higher expenditures. Therefore, if you read those reports of the parliamentary bodies which are not reprinted in all newspapers, you will find that most members of Parliament, of any parliament—I am not talking about the parliaments of the countries represented in this room—are very quick to suggest additional expenditures and to suggest additional taxes of the kinds which the voters in their district do *not* pay. At the same time, they have some inhibitions with regard to what they consider as the unjust overburdening of their own voters with taxes.

I once heard a government official, the minister of finance of a country which was famous for its inflation and not for anything else, say, "My minister of education says he needs more money. I am the minister of finance. I have to provide the money. I have to print the money." It doesn't matter whether the purpose is a good one or a bad one. What it brings about is that there is now on the market an additional demand for commodities and services which was created out of nothing.

An increase in the quantity of many things is very good—yes, an increase in the supply of those things which are useful. But an increase in the supply of, let us say rats and mice, would not be very useful. Fortunately this is not a problem men have to decide because the interests of all people agree in this regard. But their interests do not agree with regard to money. What misleads the thinking of many people, and unfortunately also the thinking of those people who are operating our governmental and political activities, is the idea that the quantity of money counts. It is certainly better for the individual to have more money than less. But it is not better for the whole economic system to have more money than less. Money is a medium of exchange. And that means, first of all, that its *quantity* is without any importance for the perfection of its functions. If you increase the total quantity of money, the total quantity of the medium of exchange, you do not improve conditions generally; you only change exchange ratios between the individuals' evaluations of goods and services and of the thing used as money. I want to make this clearer by pointing to a very simple case taken from daily affairs.

The most outspoken defender and preacher of inflation in our age, Lord Keynes, was right *from his point of view* when he attacked what is called "Say's Law." Now Say's Law is one of the great achievements of the early days of economic theory. The Frenchman, Jean-Baptiste Say,[1] in the so-called Say's Law, said you can't improve conditions by increasing the quantity of money generally; when business is not good, it is not because there isn't enough money. What Say had in mind, what he said when he criticized the doctrine that there should be more money, was that everything that somebody produces is at the same time a demand for other things. If there are more shoes produced, these shoes are something that is offered on the market in exchange for other goods. Ultimately goods are not exchanged against money—money is only a medium of exchange—goods are exchanged against other commodities. And if you increase the quantity of money you do not improve anybody's situation except the definite man to whom you give it; this man can then buy more, can then withdraw more things from the market.

When people asked a grocer, "Why is your business not better? Why don't you make more money?" he answered: "People don't have enough money and, therefore, my business is not satisfactory." What he meant was not that *all* people didn't have enough money but that his customers didn't have enough money. He said, "My customers unfortunately have not enough money and, therefore, they can't buy more from me." If the grocer wanted to earn more, and if his customers, all taken together, were not rich enough to give him more business, it would have been necessary for him to find more customers. But this grocer did not mean that more money in general was needed. He does not say he is interested in the whole world, in everybody's money. What this grocer has in mind is more money to *his* customers. This is "the grocer philosophy."

Now the governments believe, perhaps they are innocent in this as this belief is relayed to them by "bad" professors, that there is something which ought to be done. Really everybody agrees that there should be more money for this or that purpose—whether it is for schools or hospitals or scientific research or whatever doesn't make any difference. Let us say the government says that the government employees have very small salaries; they should get higher salaries. As the government itself does not produce anything, the only successful method for the government to follow is to tax the people and use the revenue collected by taxes for increasing the salaries of certain government employees. There is no possibility for the government to improve the conditions of government employees in any other way than by taking money away from the rest of the population

[1] Jean-Baptiste Say (1767–1832)

and, therefore, impairing their conditions. If the government taxes, takes away something from the taxpayers, then they are forced to restrict their expenditures but there is no reason for general price changes. Those people to whom the government gives the higher salaries are in a position to buy what the other people used to buy and can no longer buy because they had to pay the taxes. Changes would result from the fact that some things which taxpayer Mr. A used to buy are now bought no longer by Mr. A but by government employee Mr. B. This would tend to increase some prices of the things Mr. B buys and to reduce the prices asked for the things Mr. A can no longer buy. But no revolutionary change takes place in the general height of prices. This is what goes on continually in a country the government of which has a balanced budget. But there is another way, another method. And the government uses this other method.

The government prints the additional money. As you know it is very easy for the government to print money. And if the government prints this money, what is the effect? The effect is that those to whom the government gives this new money, in this instance government employees, are now in a position to buy more. Nothing has changed in the world; everything is as it was yesterday; there are no more goods available; but there is more money today because the government made it and gave it to certain government employees, let us say armaments workers. It may be for the best possible purpose. We do not discuss the items in the government budget, but only the total amount. And now the government gives money to some people, and these people appear on the markets with an additional demand, with a demand that didn't exist yesterday. Lord Keynes was enthusiastic about this demand, you know; he thought it was wonderful; yes, it is true. He called this increasing demand bringing about "effective demand." Of course, this is a very correct description. But the thing is that prices are going up. But what does it mean?

Let us take potatoes as the example. There are no more potatoes on the market. But there is more money in the hands of the people who want to eat potatoes. While yesterday it was enough for a man to spend one dollar to buy potatoes for his need, today he needs more. He needs today, let us say, two dollars, only because there is more money, not because anything else has changed. If he were only to offer one dollar, then the man who got the additional money from the government would say, "Ho, ho! I will pay $1.10 and I will get the potatoes and you can go home empty-handed." And this is the thing we all are experiencing today—price increases due to inflation.

The government increases the quantity of money. All the evils under which we are suffering in our market conditions everyday are due to the fact that governments believe that it is permissible and natural to produce money to increase the power of the government to spend. In order to spend more, the governments have to do practically nothing but give an order to a printing office: "Print a quantity of money and give it to us." If private citizens do this, the government doesn't like it. There are many printing offices in the country; most of these printing offices are in the position to print dollar bills. What prevents the individual citizen from printing dollar bills, banknotes, is a series of laws which make this a crime, and the government is powerful enough to prevent it by arresting the people and imprisoning them, and so on. But if the government itself prints additional dollars, then it is legal and it increases the quantity of money. And this is the monetary problem. Apart from the fact that this brings about a very bad situation for those people who were not receivers of the new additional money, because they have not received more money, they now face higher prices.

CHAPTER
FOURTEEN

Two Monetary Problems

The function of the government is to prevent violence. The function which the government adopted, accepted, and held with respect to money, was to say what the parties had meant and whether or not the parties to the agreement had done what they were bound to do according to the agreement which they had voluntarily accepted. In these agreements the term "money" was used in order to specify the medium of exchange used by the parties when they met, when they made the contract. But when the government faced this situation they adopted the privilege of coining the metal used in these agreements and using the coins, at first without any bad intentions. At the beginning this didn't mean anything more than the government's declaration that the coin was a piece of metal of a definite weight and that it could be used as such by the parties. But again and again in various nations, governments misused the position which this situation gave them. The situation was simply this. Already in very ancient times, in the history of almost every group of nations and of every civilization there developed among governments that did this, that coined certain pieces of metal, the idea that they had the right to—it is very difficult for me to say this word—"swindle." If one talks about all these things, one must not forget that they did it with a bad conscience. But when government got involved with money it led to two problems.

The first problem, the one which is not recognized as a monetary problem by the government, by official spokesmen and writers, is that of the increase in prices, the so-called "inflation." One of the most important features of the "New Economics,"[1] once simply known as "bad economics,"

[1] The doctrine derived primarily from the teachings of the British John Maynard Keynes

is the change in the meaning of terms. Not so long ago, "inflation" meant a considerable increase in the quantity of money and money substitutes in circulation. The effect of such an increase was always a general tendency for prices to move upward. Everybody knew this and admitted it and certainly the government knew it too. Today the terminology, the official terminology, has been changed. We have to realize that the term "inflation" is used today in popular discussions of the subject in a way which is very different from the meaning attached to it in the past. People now call the increase in prices "inflation," while in fact inflation is not the increase in prices but the increase in the quantity of money that brings about the increase in prices.

People nowadays don't talk about the increase in the quantity of money; this is a subject that the representatives of our official doctrine do not wish to mention. They speak only of the fact that prices are moving upward. This, the effect, they call "inflation." They do not mention at all the preceding fact, the *cause* of the upward movement, the increase in the quantity of money. They imply that government has nothing to do with it, that government wants only to keep prices stable. They simply assume that the upward movement of prices and wages, which they call "inflation," is caused by the wickedness of people outside government, by "bad people" who are asking higher prices.

The second problem is the actual increase in the quantity of money itself. Let us talk about a fantastically small country, let us say Ruritania. Its government wants to raise money for some of its expenses. The government says, for instance, certain workers should get higher salaries. The total amount of government taxes is one million units of the monetary unit. Yes. But the government wants to spend two millions. The government adds to the million units it has taxed away from the citizens a second million which it has printed especially for this purpose. The result is that an increased quantity of money is exchanged on the market against a not-increased quantity of real goods, of consumers goods, and so on. And this means that prices must necessarily go up. The government has a group of learned men who try to conceal this very simple relation by using terms that sometimes mean nothing and sometimes mean precisely the opposite of what is really going on in the economic system.

To realize what this means we must first ask some questions: What are the necessary and unavoidable effects of an increase in the quantity of

---

that inflation through government spending was the solution for any economic downturn. —**BBG** money? What is the effect of government's spending more than it collects in taxes or borrows from the people by increasing the quantity of money? What is the effect on prices when those who receive some of this increased quantity of money spend it?

We shouldn't be very strict in judging the governments which increase the quantity of money because they want to spend more than they collect from the people. The situation in Parliament, Congress, or the parliamentary body is that there is, on the one hand, a very unpopular tax, very unpopular, and on the other side there is a very popular expenditure. You know government expenditures are always popular with those people who receive the money the government spends. Now this is a fact, you know; you can't change it. There is a very popular expenditure. And elections are not far away. Now what does the government do in such a situation, a weak government? Don't say that if you were in control, you would have a better government; perhaps you would also be weak if you were in this situation. The government resorts to inflation, and that means an increase in the quantity of money. And this is the second monetary problem.

CHAPTER
FIFTEEN

Deficit Financing and Credit Expansion

I assume that you know how the banking system developed and how the banks could improve the services rendered by gold by transferring assets from one individual to another individual in the books of the banks. When you study the development of the history of money you will discover that there were countries in which there were systems in which all the payments were made by transactions in the books of a bank, or of several banks. The individuals acquired an account by paying gold into this bank. There is a limited quantity of gold so the payments which are made are limited. And it was possible to transfer gold from the account of one man to the account of another. But then the governments began something which I can only describe in general words. The governments began to issue paper which they wanted to serve the role, perform the service, of money. When people bought something they expected to receive from their bank a certain quantity of gold to pay for it. But the government asked: What's the difference whether the people really get gold or whether they get a title from the bank that gives them the right to ask for gold? It will be all the same to them. So the government issued paper notes, or gave the bank the privilege to issue paper notes, which gave the receiver the right to ask for gold. This led to an increase in the number of paper banknotes which gave to the bearer the right to ask for gold.

Not too long ago our government proclaimed a new method for making everybody prosperous: a method called "deficit financing." Now that is a wonderful word. You know, technical terms have the bad habit of not being understood by people. The government and the journalists who were writing for the government told us about this "deficit spending." It was wonderful! It was considered something that would improve conditions in the whole country. But if you translate this into more common language, the language of the uneducated, then you say "printed money." The government says this is only due to your lack of education; if you had an education you wouldn't say "printed money;" you would call it "deficit financing" or "deficit spending." Now what does this mean? Deficits! This means that the government spends more than it collects in taxes and in borrowing from the people; it means government spending for all those purposes for which the government wants to spend. This means inflation, pushing more money into the market; it doesn't matter for what purpose. And that means reducing the purchasing power of each monetary unit. Instead of collecting the money that the government wanted to spend, the government fabricated the money. Printing money is the easiest thing. Every government is clever enough to do it.

If the government wants to pay out more money than before, if it wants to buy more commodities for some purpose or to raise the salaries of government employees, no other way is open to it under normal conditions than to collect more taxes and use this increased income to pay, for instance, for the higher wages of its employees. The fact that people have to pay higher taxes so that the government may pay higher wages to its employees means that individual taxpayers are forced to restrict their expenditures. This restriction of purchases on the part of the taxpayers counteracts the expansion of purchases by those receiving the money collected by the government. Thus, this simple contraction of spending on the part of some, the taxpayers from whom money is taken to give to others, does not bring about a general change in prices.

The thing is that the individual cannot do anything that makes the inflationary machine and mechanism work. This is done by the government. The government makes the inflation. And if the government complains about the fact that prices are going up and appoints committees of learned men to fight against the inflation, we have only to say: "Nobody other than you, the government brings about inflation, you know."

On the other hand, if the government does not raise taxes, does not increase its normal revenues, but prints an additional quantity of money and distributes it to government employees, additional buyers appear on the market. The number of buyers is increased as a result while the quantity of goods offered for sale remains the same. Prices necessarily go up, because there are more people with more money asking for commodities which had not increased in supply. The government does not speak of the increase in the quantity of money as "inflation;" it calls the fact that commodity prices are going up "inflation." The government then asks who is responsible for this "inflation," that is for the higher prices? The answer—"bad" people; they may not know why prices are going up but nevertheless they are sinning by asking for higher prices.

The best proof that inflation, the increase in the quantity of money, is very bad is the fact that those who are making the inflation are denying again and again, with the greatest fervor, that they are responsible. "Inflation?" they ask. "Oh! This is what *you* are doing because you are asking higher prices. We don't know why prices are going up. There are bad people who are making the prices go up. But not the government!" And the government says: "Higher prices? Look, these people, this corporation, this bad man, the president of this corporation, . . ." Even if the government blames the unions—I don't want to talk about the unions—but even then we have to realize what the unions *cannot* do is to increase the quantity of money. And, therefore, all the activities of the unions are within the framework that is built by the government in influencing the quantity of money.

The situation, the political situation, the discussion of the problem of inflation, would be very different if the people who are making the inflation, the government, were openly saying, "Yes, we do it. We are making the inflation. Unfortunately we have to spend more than people are prepared to pay in taxes." But they don't say this. They do not even say openly to everybody, "We have increased the quantity of money. We are increasing the quantity of money because we are spending more, more than you are paying us." And this leads us to a problem which is purely political.

Those into whose pockets the additional money goes first profit from the situation, whereas others are compelled to restrict their expenditures. The government does not acknowledge this; it does not say, "We have increased the quantity of money and, therefore, prices are going up." The government starts by saying, "Prices are going up. Why? Because people are bad. It is the duty of the government to prevent bad people from bringing about this upward movement of prices, this inflation. Who can do this? The government!" Then the government says: "We will prevent profiteering, and all these things. *These* people, the profiteers are the ones who are making inflation; they are asking higher prices." And the government elaborates "guidelines" for those who do not wish to be in wrong with the government. Then, it adds that this is due to "inflationary pressures." They have invented many other terms also which I cannot remember, such silly terms, to describe this situation—"cost-push inflation," "inflationary pressures," and the like. Nobody knows what an "inflationary pressure" is; it has never been defined.[1] What *is* clear is what inflation is.

Inflation is a considerable addition to the quantity of money in circulation. This upward movement of prices due to the inflation, due to the fact that the system was inflated by additional quantities of money, brings the prices up. And this system can work for some time, but only if there is some power that restricts the government's wish to expand the quantity of money and is powerful enough to succeed to some extent in this regard. The evils which the government, its helpers, its committees, and so on, acknowledge are connected with this inflation, but not in the way in which they are discussed. This shows that the intention of the governments and of its propagators (propagandizers, promoters) is to conceal the real cause of what is happening. If we want to have a money that is acceptable on the market as the medium of exchange, it must be something that cannot be increased with a profit by anybody, whether government or a citizen. *The worst failures of money, the worst things done to money were not done by criminals but by governments, which very often ought to be considered, by and large, as ignoramuses but not as criminals.*

[1] Talk of "inflationary pressures" and "guidelines" dates from the 1960s. At that time, business firms were raising prices and wage rates because the government had expanded the nation's quantity of money so much and government officials were trying to persuade private business firms to keep price and wage increases below 3.2%. This was the maximum considered permissible "under the President's voluntary guidelines [or "guideposts"] for non-inflationary wage and price hikes." And President Johnson threatened a tax increase if "inflationary pressures" did not cease. See *World Almanac, 1967*, pp. 60, 61. —**BBG**

CHAPTER
SIXTEEN

Credit Expansion and the Trade Cycle

Now what is credit expansion? Credit expansion is inflation also. The reason for making a distinction between credit expansion and simple inflation is because of the different effects that an additional quantity of money has upon entering the economic system by the two different routes. In simple inflation, the new money enters by spending on the part of government. The government spends additional sums created, for instance, for the purpose of carrying on a war. The effect of this spending is that prices of the things the government buys go up and consumers start to hoard. With credit expansion the additional quantities of money enter the economic system, not through government spending, but through loans of newly created credit to businessmen by the banks. So the prices of the things businesses buy go up. This brings about a "boom" in business. If this boom is not stopped in time, it develops into a great economic crisis. This is the trade cycle, the most interesting phenomenon of the capitalistic system.

The trade cycle is due to the fact that banks expand credit and this credit expansion brings about an expansion of business. But as the quantities of producers' goods, capital goods, are not increased, there is an over-expansion of some businesses, but not a general over-investment, as it is called by some finance brokers, throughout the whole economy. The significant characteristic of the boom is this over-expansion by the artificial lowering of the interest rate in order to create the credit expansion. This misleads businessmen into thinking that there is a greater amount of capital goods available than actually exists, and that certain projects are now possible which would have been impossible with a higher rate of interest. In fact the only thing that is newly available is an increased amount of credit created precisely for this purpose. This system, this "boom," goes on until finally it breaks down when it becomes apparent that the so-called "over-investment" is actually *mal-investment* or over-expansion in some areas of the economy.

Nevertheless, we have a situation now in which each of the leading countries of the world wants to expand, to have a lower rate of interest. People have always been hostile to interest as such, considering it "usury." The idea has long prevailed that the interest rate is something that can be manipulated *ad libitum* [at will] by government and the banks. The reason for this attitude is a misunderstanding of the whole modern economic system. What makes very great problems is the wish of all countries, or let us say of the inflationists of all countries, to have a lower rate of interest. What I am concerned with at this time is the effects this tendency on the part of each country has on market prices, savings and investment.

If the countries have an international currency, or if they have national currencies which are free from gold, people will be in favor of increasing the quantity of money. Few people are in favor of decreasing the quantity of money and falling prices. If a government wants to become popular, it will try to raise the prices for the benefit of the consumers, for the benefit of the producers, and especially for the benefit of the unions. There will, therefore, be a tendency toward an increase in the quantity of money. An increase in the quantity of money brings about higher prices. And if there is a tendency toward higher prices there is also necessarily a tendency for interest rates to go up. Recently a columnist wrote in a leading weekly that we have tamed the business cycle. Perhaps you read his column—I read it just an hour before leaving for this meeting. But really, there is nothing to tame unless it be the inflationists, those who want to hold interest rates low and expand credit artificially, those who do not think that conditions, as determined by the savings of people, are satisfactory.

Interest rates must go up when there is a general tendency for prices to go up because, if you buy commodities instead of lending money and hold the commodities, you make an extra profit in such a situation by the increase in the prices of the commodities you have bought. Therefore, people will prefer not to lend money to anybody if there is not an indemnification in the rate of interest which they are receiving for the profit they could make by buying commodities or stocks themselves and keeping them for a time until their prices went up. Therefore, the state of affairs in which prices are going up is necessarily a state of affairs in which the rate of interest will go up also, because under such conditions the rate of interest must contain an element which I have called the "price premium," that is an indemnification for the profit the money lender could earn himself by buying commodities instead of giving a loan.

Now when the rates of interest are going up, people will say that what is needed to fight the high rate of interest is to increase the quantity of money. But the situation is precisely the opposite. The only method to have lower interest rates is not to have inflation, to remove from the power of the government the problem of increasing or decreasing the quantity of money. The government will always be in favor of inflation, because governments always want to spend more. Therefore, there will be general disagreement about policies.

The beginnings of the inflation are always characterized by the fact that those who are favored by the inflation are the first to declare that conditions are very good and that they want the government to continue. The government wants to be able to say to the voters, to the people, "You never had such a wonderful time as you are enjoying now." And such a wonderful time can very easily be brought about for a very short time by inflation, you know. Only later do people discover what the results are. And only later do they discover that this means, at the same time, the destruction of the savings of all those people who are not themselves owners of some real property or some enterprise.

CHAPTER
SEVENTEEN

Balance of Payments Doctrine, Purchasing Power Parity and Foreign Trade

If a government doesn't know what to do, it wants to "bribe" people by paying something to them, paying without having collected by taxation the means required for this payment. And this is what the governments are doing. This is inflation, you know. Everywhere today you hear the governments talk about inflation. They describe inflation as higher prices, as something that happens—one doesn't know why. Or, according to another version, they say that it is due to the activities of some people, to the bad actions of people. The people are responsible. Let us take the most popular case, the problem of foreign exchange. We have today a situation in which the various governments in their inflationary measures do not act in concert. That means, one government goes farther in its inflationary measures than others. And therefore, there are continual changes in the mutual exchange ratios of the various countries' governmental money.

What the government that embarks upon inflation does not want to admit is that the paper money that it has issued is in any way less valuable than the money which it wants to replace. We have, in fact now all over the world, inflation. We have also inflation in this country, and tremendous deficits in the budget that are covered by the issuance of additional new paper money. And the government maintains that this has nothing to do with monetary problems.

What we have to realize is that on the market, on all markets without any exception, whether they are domestic markets or whether it is the world market, there prevails the purchasing power parity principle. This is a fundamental principle of the market. It means there prevails a tendency toward the equalization of exchange ratios between the various commodities and money—between the commodities themselves, between the commodities and money, and between the various kinds of money circulating in the world. This is the interpretation, the correct interpretation of what is going on in connection between the various commodities.

If there is a deviation from this purchasing power parity, then there is a way open for businessmen to make profits. And the purpose of all transactions on the market is to make such occasions to earn profits disappear by buying in one currency and selling in another currency. It is impossible for a state of affairs to remain in which such differences between the purchasing powers of the various currencies could prevail. As far as the governments try to make such exchanges impossible there is an end of business, an end of buying and selling, but not an equalization of the prices expressed in the various currencies of the world. Therefore, it is impossible for a country or a government to prevent the devaluation of its currency, if this currency is being increased, without preserving its parity against the original money with which the government pretends the parity still exists. All this means finally that the gold standard alone, the full and pure gold standard, is free from government interference with prices and with the value of all those items that are expressed in terms of money.

When our monetary problems are discussed, you never hear the representatives of the government or the official economists of all these committees that are established for this purpose refer to the fact that there is deficit spending, that there is an increase in the quantity of money. And if there are some problems to deal with, the lower valuation, the lower purchasing power, of the government-issued money as against the money which it was once thought to represent, the gold money, then the governments, and also first of all the American government and its advisors, refer to a doctrine that has been discredited long, long ago—the balance of payments doctrine. I don't want to give the history of this doctrine, nor to demonstrate how it was discredited. I want rather to analyze the remedy that the government has suggested for healing the monetary evils, the remedy from the point of view of the balance of payments doctrine.

In the eyes of the government, the evil is the lower valuation of the government-issued money as against the money which it was once thought to represent. And this, they say, is due to the fact that there are some very "bad citizens" in the country who are spending "our money"—I want to put "our money" in quotation marks. People who are using "our money" are squandering "our money" in order to buy absolutely bad commodities abroad—in France champagne and other French wines, for instance. And the remedy recommended is to make it impossible by acts of legislation for these people to use "our money"—again in quotation marks—for the purchase of such useless things as French wines. They say the reason why prices expressed in dollars and prices expressed in other currencies are going up is due to you, the people. The people are responsible, according to the governments, because they are drinking imported champagne and because they are traveling in foreign countries. Why do they speak about champagne and about traveling in foreign countries? Because, as the governments consider it, these are luxury things. Therefore, what the government does is simply, "Look at these bad people who are drinking champagne. They are responsible for the inflation, for the higher prices; they are responsible for all evils under the sun." The way in which the American government deals with the problem is only one of the ways in which the government justifies its action. This is "the luxury excuse."

But there is a second excuse, "the necessities of life" excuse, which countries give when imports consist predominantly of goods that are considered, by public opinion, as necessary and indispensable. In such countries—for instance, in all those European countries that are predominantly industrial, exporting industrial products, manufactures, in order to import food and raw materials. They say: "What is responsible for our unfavorable development of foreign exchange rates is the fact that we are poor insofar as we cannot produce on our own territory all the foodstuffs and raw materials needed and we have to import them. These other nations, the 'have' nations, are exploiting us." This is the version which, for instance, was used by Mussolini in order to justify *his* aggression: "Why must we go to war against other countries? Because we are forced to import things which are absolutely necessary for the support of the life and health, and so on, of our population."

What the government does *not* say—when it blames the balance of payments for the effect of inflation on the purchasing power parity—is that if people are prevented from spending dollars to import champagne, they would buy something else. They would not put the dollars in a package and send this package to the government so it would have more money for paying the deficits of its enterprises, the post office, for instance. If instead of buying imported champagne, they are buying other things on the domestic market, the prices of those things would go up on account of the fact that there is now a greater demand for them. This will bring about higher prices for some things which previously were exported. And those things would become more expensive, less available and would no longer be exported. If the governments were consistent, or *could* be consistent in this regard, they would make all imports impossible and prevent all business with foreign countries; they would necessarily restrict exports to the same extent that they are restricting imports and this would bring about restriction, the complete end of international trade. And every country would remain isolated economically.

Now why does this bad balance of payments situation develop only between national units and not within the national unit? In Europe, there are several governments, or several nations, the population of which is either smaller or not much larger than the population of many American states. Why don't you hear the same complaints about the various American states which you hear about the comportment of some people who are buying champagne and are therefore enriching France and impoverishing the United States? Because the various American states of the union do not have an independent monetary policy; there cannot be inflation in Iowa that is not at the same time and to the same extent also an inflation in the 49 other states of the union. And you need not go to the states. When people say what is bad in the relationship between the United States and France is that France produces and sells to the United States only goods which are very frivolous, very bad, immoral goods—books, novels, theatrical performances, opera productions and concerts in Paris, and champagne which is the worst of all things—you could say the same thing also about, let us say, Brooklyn and Manhattan. Manhattan sells theatrical performances, conferences, concerts, and so on, in greater numbers to the people from Brooklyn while these people of Brooklyn are spending money in Manhattan. Typically, a man in Brooklyn might say: "Why does my neighbor spend his money to attend the performance of an opera in Manhattan? Why does he not spend his money in Brooklyn?" And if you go step by step farther in the same direction, you arrive at perfect autarky, self-sufficiency, isolation, economic isolation of every individual family and perhaps even within the family. Why should not a boy, as opposed to his brother or sister or his parents, say consequently and consistently "I want to be autarkic" for the same reasons that one of the countries in the world wants to be autarkic and prevent the importing of things from other countries.

Now let us analyze what will be the effect of such a measure—preventing Americans from importing French wine, champagne, or otherwise. It will certainly bring about an impairment of the business of the

French producers of wine. And the prices which they will have to charge will have to drop in order to make it possible for them to sell all their production, their whole production, somewhere else, either in France or in other countries. They will have to sell at lower prices than those which they would have received if the Americans had bought this French product. That means that there will be in France now people who are no longer in a position to maintain the standard of living which they maintained before. They will have to restrict their consumption. They will, for instance, have to restrict purchases of imported commodities, let us say, of American cars. And in this way they will adjust themselves to the new situation. This means that when you prohibit the importation of some goods from foreign countries, you necessarily make, not only American imports decrease, but also those American exports which would have been sold in payment for these imports of French luxury goods. And this does not refer only to France. The connection is a little bit more complicated; other countries are included; the French do not only restrict their consumption of American goods, but they restrict also the importation of goods from other countries. And then these other countries are in the chain of causation which finally brings about necessarily a drop in American exports also.

If all countries of the world, consistently keeping to this balance of payments theory, were to proceed in the same way in order to make their domestic currencies independent of international valuation, i.e., their purchasing power parity, this system would finally bring an end to any kind of international trade. All imports would be prevented. And the result of stopping all imports will mean, of course, also the end of export trade. Every country will be self-sufficient, autarkic, as the Greek term says. Now there was such a period in history. Not so long ago there were many countries in the world that had no commercial relations with other countries, especially not with far distant countries. And there was once, long, long ago, a period of history in which there was no foreign trade at all. And when foreign trade developed it always meant both exporting and importing.

Foreign trade is not one-sided. It is always necessarily a mutual exchange of commodities and services between various countries. This has nothing to do with the appraisal of the purchasing power of the monetary unit. It is not the import of French wines that makes the price of domestic commodities go up. The price of these domestic commodities goes up on account of the fact that the government has increased the quantity of money and, therefore, as expressed in a very questionable way, "an increased quantity of American paper bills is now chasing a not-increased quantity of goods available for consumption." If all imports and exports were stopped, the various countries would return to autarky; they would have to forego all the advantages which result from exchange in other countries.

Now the only thing we can learn from the whole situation is this. The market, the people buying and selling on the market outside of the government, have developed in the course of centuries a system of money based on the precious metals, silver and gold. The governments interfered again and again. Government interference excluded silver from the monetary system which the market had developed, leaving only gold as money. Yet governments—the individual governments, the various governments, and now the cooperation of the various governments in the International Monetary Fund—have not succeeded yet in bringing about the demolition of this system. Whatever one says about it, one has to realize that money is a creation of the market, a creation of the people buying, selling, and producing. It is not something that the government can manipulate just to make it possible for the government to spend more than the people are prepared to pay.

CHAPTER

EIGHTEEN

Inter-bank Liquidity; Bank Reserves

Now we have another problem which is usually regarded as an ordinary monetary matter. Various government committees of professors and representatives of various central banks are studying a problem sometimes referred to as that of inter-bank liquidity, or as the problem of bank reserves. What exactly is this problem? I think the easiest way to understand this problem is to refer to the conditions as they existed in world money markets from the second half of the nineteenth century until the outbreak of the First World War. At that time the economically leading nations of the world were all on the gold or gold exchange standard and they were interested in preserving the gold parity of their domestic national currency. At the same time they wanted to maintain a low rate of interest in the money markets of their respective countries and to expand credit, to have credit expansion, in order to encourage business and bring about a "boom."

The governments became interested in entering the market and destroying the market because the governments wanted to spend money, more money than the citizens were prepared to pay. I am not talking about the United States but about almost all other countries in the world. It was for the government always a problem to tell the citizens, especially if they already were paying high taxes: "We want more money." And for what purpose? "To pay the deficits of our enterprises. Don't forget the problem of the government enterprises." In the second part of the 19th century, there was a great man, one of the most important and most influential statesmen in the world—the German Prince Bismarck, who favored nationalization. And Bismarck nationalized the Prussian railroads. Why? Because this was considered a simple thing. What do these railroad men do? The trains are running and the money was coming in. The government had said: "What a wonderful thing are the railroads. They are making lots of money. It is so easy, of course. Just set the trains running and everybody will want to go somewhere. Or they will want to ship some goods on this railroad. Therefore, the railroads are a wonderful thing. Let us nationalize the railroads and we, the government, will get their profits." So they nationalized the railroads. Bismarck was not the *only* one to do this; he was only the most important man to do it. All other countries, or most other countries, tried to do the same thing. They nationalized the telegraph, the telephone, and so on. Then there appeared something very interesting. After the railroads, that had been making profits, were nationalized, they began making deficits. And the deficits had to be paid. The citizens said, "You are nationalizing more and more. You are taxing more and more. And what is the result? More deficits!"

In this regard, let us say only parenthetically that the United States did not nationalize the railroads. But the United States pays foreign aid, subsidies, to many countries that have nationalized their railroads. The United States government collects taxes from the American railroads which, after all, still have some surpluses and not deficits, like many foreign railroads.[1] And these surpluses are used by foreign countries to pay the deficits of their nationalized railroads. Some may say it might have been better to nationalize the American railroads also and to have deficits than to pay the deficits of the foreign nationalized enterprises. We do have in this country *one* monument to this deficit system—the American Post Office: one billion dollars almost, or perhaps more—one doesn't know. But the fact that the U.S. government Post Office makes deficits serves as a warning to the U.S. government against nationalizing other industries.

In the second half of the nineteenth century, if an individual country kept the interest rate lower than it ought to be in order to increase the quantity of money and spend more, the tendency was for short term capital to move, within a very short period of time, to a foreign country. For example, if Germany, so often the evil-doer preceding the First World War, kept a very low interest rate, short term capital moved out of Germany to other countries where the interest rate was not so low. This meant people were trying to withdraw gold from Germany in order to transfer it to England, France or the United States. The Reichsbank, seeing its gold reserves dwindling and fearing it would not be able to fulfill its obligations because of its shortage of gold, was forced to go up again with the interest

[1] These lectures were delivered by Mises in the 1960s. —**BBG**

rate in order to stop the withdrawal of gold, i.e., its "gold reserves."

Not all countries inflate, or if they do inflate, they do not inflate to the same extent. Switzerland is considered a "bad" country because it does not inflate sufficiently. Therefore, there are continual problems with the flow of money from countries which have more inflation to others which have not inflated to the same extent. If the various governments and central banks do not all act in the same way, if some banks or governments go a little farther than the others, the situation develops that I have just described; those who expand more are forced to return to the market rate of interest in order to preserve their solvency through liquidity; they want to prevent funds from being withdrawn from their country; they do not want to see their reserves in gold or foreign money dwindling. And one calls this the "international problem."

In the nineteenth century one spoke of "the war of the banks." This term was not a good one. It would have been more correct to refer to the useless attempts of central banks, from time to time, to maintain a lower rate of interest within their own country than actual conditions permitted. Nevertheless, this expression, "the war of the banks," was most popular during the first decade of the present [20th] century when the Peace Conference at the Hague was in vogue. One day the Italian Minister of Finance even suggested a "peace conference" of the central banks in order to end "the war of the banks." However, there was neither a "war of the banks" nor a "peace conference" of the banks.

All countries in the past had only metallic money, no paper money, and they used the metallic money according to weight—you know the metallic weight of money still remains in the names of some monetary units, for instance the "pound sterling." Money was then valued according to its content of metal, and governments were not in a position to increase the quantity of money. But the problem of money connected with a purely metallic currency is not the problem of our age. The problem we have to meet today, what we have to face today, is that the governments pretend that they have the right to increase the quantity of money if they want to spend more. And the governments that do this, to the extent that they do, become very angry if somebody says it has adopted an inflationary policy. They say inflationary conditions are what businessmen cause by asking higher prices. But the question is not that the businessmen ask for higher prices, you know; the question is why did they not ask higher prices yesterday before the government increased the quantity of money? If they had asked higher prices yesterday, people would not have paid the higher prices because they did not have the money, and the businessmen would have been forced to lower their prices if they wanted to sell their commodities. All these things have only one cause. And all these things can be cured in only one way, by not inflating, by not supplying additional quantities of money, of the medium of exchange.

There is a proverb that says: "One doesn't talk about the gallows in the home of a family, one of whose members was executed." In this way, one doesn't talk about the international problem in terms of inflation. When one talks about an international monetary problem, one says there is not enough "liquidity," not enough "reserves."

The international monetary system of the nineteenth century, which ended with the catastrophe of the First World War, was, by and large, practically re-established after the war was over and again after the Second World War. The central banks today still want to preserve the stability of exchange rates. Therefore, their attempts to lower interest rates will create a situation which leads them to fear an external drain, with withdrawal of funds in order to transfer them to foreign countries. At such times, the Bank, the so-called monetary authorities, are faced with an alternative: either to devalue, which they do not want to do, or to go up again with the rate of interest. But the central banks like neither alternative. They complain, saying there is insufficient "liquidity" in international monetary affairs.

In order to cure this evil, to make more "liquidity," many experts have suggested the creation of a new reserve currency. If people in Belgium, let us say, want to withdraw funds from that country to transfer to Paris, they need foreign exchange—French francs or the exchange of other countries belonging to this group of several countries, not some reserve currency. A reserve currency, of course, might be a very good way out. It would mean printing more money and forcing people to accept it. And the International Monetary Fund did it, you know.[2] It is beside the point that those who attend International Monetary Fund meetings, who serve on the committees, join in discussions and write books, announce almost every week some new project or invent some new method in the hope of increasing liquidity or adding to the reserves. It is characteristic that many new names have been invented for such a new reserve currency. You read in the newspapers these wonderful stories about "paper gold." Nobody knows what paper gold is, you know. There are paper cigarettes, but pa-

[2]In 1969 the IMF created Special Drawing Rights, sometimes called "paper gold," intended to supplement existing bank reserves. —**BBG**

per gold is something which the government promises.[3] It is necessary to abandon all ideas of an artificial currency and all those silly ideas about paper gold, gold paper. However, the name is not really important. The fact is that it is useless and hopeless for one country to try and keep a rate of interest lower than the international situation permits.

In the nineteenth century the slogan of those excellent British economists who were titans at criticizing socialistic enthusiasts, was: "There is but one method of relieving the conditions of the future generations of the masses, and that is to accelerate the formation of capital as against the increase of population." Since then, there has taken place a tremendous increase in population, for which the silly term "population explosion" was invented. However, we are not having a "capital explosion," only an "explosion" of wishes and an "explosion" of futile attempts to substitute something else—fiat money or credit money—for money.

[3]When a member of Mises' audience once asked him what he thought of "paper gold," he responded, "You should ask the alchemists." —**BBG**

CHAPTER

NINETEEN

Does the World Need a World Bank and More Money?

As a medium of exchange, the situation of money is different from that of other commodities. If there is an increase in the quantity of other commodities, this always means an improvement of conditions for people. For instance, if there is more wheat available, some people for whom there was no wheat available before can now get some, or they can get more than they would have received under the previous conditions. But with money the situation is very different.

To point this out, you have only to consider what happens if there is an increase in the quantity of money. Such an increase is considered bad because it favors those who get the new money first at the expense of others; it never happens in such a way as to leave relations among individuals unchanged. Let us take the following situation. Imagine the world as our world is, you know. Some people own money and also claims on money, claims to get money from somebody else; they are creditors. Then there are also people who are debtors, who have debts in money. Now imagine a second world which is precisely the same as the first world except for one thing, that wherever there is a quantity of money available, a cash holding, or a demand for money in the first world, there is in the second world the double of it. That means that everything is the same in both worlds, nothing is changed except something in the arithmetic. Everything in the second world is multiplied by two. Then you will say, "It doesn't make any difference for me whether I live in the first world or the second world. Conditions are the same." However, if changes in the supply of money were to bring this about, one might think that this also was only a problem of arithmetic, a problem for accountants; the accountants would have to use other figures, but it would not change relations among individuals. It would be absolutely uninteresting, immaterial, for people whether they were living in a world with larger or smaller figures to be used for accounting and bookkeeping. But the way money changes actually occur in our living world does not correspond to this. *The way in which changes in the quantity of money are really brought about in the world is different for different people for different things; the changes do not occur in a neutral way; some people gain at the expense of others.* That means, therefore, that if the quantity of money is increased or doubled it affects different people differently. It means also that an increase in the quantity of money doesn't bring any general improvement of conditions. This is what the French economist Say pointed out very clearly at the beginning of the 19th century.

We could deal with this problem from the point of view of the world market and the World Bank. Assume that there are some people who think that the best solution for the monetary problem would be a world paper currency, issued by a world bank or a world institution, a world office, and so on. And now assume we have such a thing. Many people want to have it. They think it would be a wonderful idea. There would be somewhere, possibly in China, an office for the whole world. And this office alone would increase the quantity of money. Yes! But who would get this additional quantity of money? There is no method of distribution which would be satisfactory to everybody. Or let us say that the international bank issuing a world money for all countries wants to increase the quantity of money because, they say, there are now more people born. All right; give it to them. But then the question is who gets the additional money? Everybody, every country, would say the same thing: "The quantity we got is too small for us." The rich countries will say, "As the per head quota of money in our country is greater than it is in the poor countries, we must get a greater part." The poor country will say, "No, on the contrary. Because they have already a greater part of money per head quota than we have, *we* must get the additional quantity of money." Therefore, all these discussions of, let us say the Bretton Woods Conference [1944], were absolutely useless because they did not even approach the situation in which they could deal with the real problem which, as far as I think, none of the delegates and none of the home governments that had sent these delegates even understood. There will be a tendency toward higher prices in those countries that are getting this additional quantity and those who receive it first will be in a position to pay higher prices. So other people will want more, you know. And the higher prices will withdraw commodities and services from the other nations which did not get this new money or not a sufficient quantity of it.

It is very easy to write in a textbook saying that the money should be increased every year by 5% or 10% and so on. Nobody talks of decreasing the quantity of money; they want only to increase it. People say: "As economic production—or the population—is increasing, one needs more and more money, more liquidity." I want to repeat what I said which is very important; there is no way of increasing—or of decreasing—the quantity of money in a neutral way. This is one of the great mistakes that is very popular. And this will bring about a struggle between all countries, or groups of countries, for whatever the units of this system will be.

But one *doesn't* need more and more money generally. And if one increases the money, one can never increase the quantity in a neutral way, in such a way that it does not further the economic conditions of one group at the expense of other groups. This is, for instance, something that wasn't realized in this great error—I don't find a nice word to describe it—in starting the International Monetary Fund. Even that dreadful ignoramus who was called Lord Keynes had not the slightest idea of it. Neither did the other people. It was not all his fault—why did they permit him to do this?

It is impossible to have a money that is only government-made, made by the world government, if it is not once and for all limited in its quantity. And limiting the quantity of money is not something which those who are suggesting these things want to happen. Such a state of affairs cannot prevail. In regard to a money, which unlike the gold standard is not increased except as it is increased by the given situation of gold mining, increasing its quantity is not only a quantitative problem; it is, first of all, a problem of *to whom* this increase should be given. Therefore, all those ideas that one could bring about a world currency completely produced and operated by some world institution is simply based upon a complete misunderstanding, ignorance of the problem of the non-neutrality of money, of the fact that increases or additions to the money cannot be dealt with in a way which will be acknowledged by all people as a "just" distribution.

CHAPTER
TWENTY

Conclusion

We must realize that money can operate, it can work, only if we have a system in which the government is prevented from manipulating the value of the money. We need not ask whether it is better to have a money with a higher or a lower purchasing power per unit. What we must realize is that we ought not to have a system of money in which the value of the monetary unit is in the hands of the government so that the government can operate, manipulate the money market in the way it wants to.

If the government destroys the monetary system it destroys perhaps the most important foundation of inter-human economic cooperation. What we have to avoid is permitting the government to increase the quantity of money as it wants. You will ask why do I not say we should keep the government from decreasing it. Of course, they shouldn't decrease the money supply either. But there is no danger that this will be done. The government will not want to do that because that would be expensive; it would have to tax, collect money from the people, and then not spend it, but destroy it. What is necessary is to prevent government from destroying the monetary system by inflating. Therefore the quantity of money shouldn't be manipulated by the government, according to the wishes of those people who want to enjoy a few minutes, a few hours, a few days, or a few weeks of good life from increased government spending, for a very long disastrous state of affairs.

The fundamental issue of money is that it must be something that cannot be increased by anybody *ad libitum*. The fight by governments against money had begun already long before the invention of the printing press by Gutenberg. But at that time the method was different. The method was by coin clipping, currency debasement, mixing into the silver coins a cheaper metal such as copper. Inflation is much easier now with the printing press. It doesn't make any difference for the government in its cost of production whether it produces a one dollar bill or a thousand dollar bill. The paper and quantities of other materials are precisely the same.

Briefly, we have to say that if a government collects all that it spends by taxing the people, and if the constitutional conditions are such that the taxpayers themselves must give the government the right to collect taxes and the government is prevented from taxing, from levying any taxes that are not legally based upon the consent of the people, then we could hope that conditions would develop in such a way that later generations would enjoy a more, let us say, civilized and comfortable life than their ancestors did and that conditions would improve considerably. We could then say the conditions were better because many evils for which older generations had no remedy were no longer such evils. We could then really speak about progress. But if we have inflation, progressing inflation, then we are continually working against the vital interests of the majority of the population.

We are very proud to acknowledge the progress of technology and especially of medical technology in the course of the last centuries which has made conditions much more tolerable for a great part of the population so that today people are no longer hurt by deficiencies and problems which were really very bad dangers for the life and health of people 20, 100, 200 years ago. However by inflating we are creating a situation which will discourage the saving and investment that made technological progress possible. At the same time by inflating, people who are getting older are continually being punished by loss of the purchasing power of the reserves they have accumulated for their own old age and for family circumstances as they will develop in the course of time. We have to realize also that such an inflation is the necessary result of the financial policies adopted by most of the governments of the world today.

What we may say has been said again and again. Theoretically also it would be possible to have a paper currency created by the government without inflation. Perhaps! But we must realize that it is not to blame the statesmen and the members of parliamentary bodies that have to determine these things when we say they are not angels. If they were angels, one could trust that they would never make any mistakes. But for common men there remains—and this is the great problem—the dilemma to which I have referred before: *the dilemma between a very unpopular tax and a very popular expenditure on the eve of an election campaign*!

While people are talking about many things as bad and making suggestions concerning the improvement of many conditions, they do not realize that there is one factor which brings about, not only an impairment of economic conditions for the greater part of the population, but also destroys the political scene by continually creating new causes of unrest. That is inflation. But it is clear that the governments who are responsible for the inflation always want to blame other people, to find that the actions of other people, not their own actions, brought about the inflation.

We must say that what creates the inflation is the famous "remedy" for the government's problems, the "remedy" which people believed was discovered some few years ago, but which was really discovered by the Roman emperors—deficit spending. Deficit spending made it possible for the government to spend more money than it had and that it collected from the people. As everybody knows, deficit spending, that is spending more than one's income, is very bad for the individual. The great error is that people believe that what is bad for the individual is not necessarily also bad for all the individuals together. This is the great mistake. And if this mistake is not eliminated very soon, all our technological and scientific improvements will not prevent us from a tremendous financial catastrophe that will destroy practically all that civilization has created in the last several hundred years.

What we have to deal with today is the fact that with a strict gold standard and gold exchange standard, we can arrange conditions in a way in which this metal gold can be used as a medium of exchange. What if you or somebody asked, what would you have suggested if there had not been any gold and any silver in the world? What would you have suggested? There is a very simple answer to this. The answer is that gold and silver are not necessarily the only media that can perform the function of a monetary system *if people realize that the quantity of money must be strictly limited by some method.* We have now no such other method.

As we see the situation today, even the most powerful, most moral, I would say, the most intellectual governments of the world—even if I were to ascribe all these attributes to the American government—are not prepared to resist inflation, to go away from increasing the quantity of money.

Printed in Great Britain
by Amazon

41211447R00056